Edited by NEIL SPILLER

AHMM

CONSTRUCTING
A PRACTICE

AHMM,
White Collar Factory,
Old Street,
London,
2017

AHMM, The Fifth Man, Bartlett
School of Architecture, University
College London (UCL), 1986

ISSN 0003-8504
ISBN 978 1119 717485

Edited by **Neil Spiller**

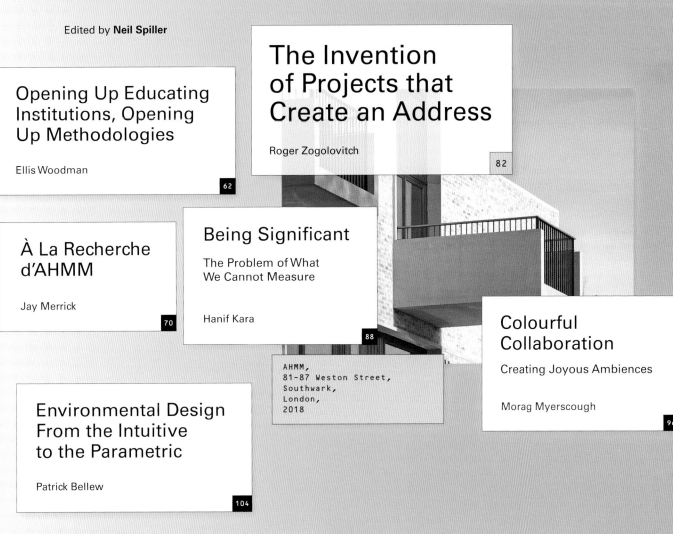

Opening Up Educating Institutions, Opening Up Methodologies

Ellis Woodman

62

The Invention of Projects that Create an Address

Roger Zogolovitch

82

À La Recherche d'AHMM

Jay Merrick

70

Being Significant

The Problem of What We Cannot Measure

Hanif Kara

88

```
AHMM,
81-87 Weston Street,
Southwark,
London,
2018
```

Colourful Collaboration

Creating Joyous Ambiences

Morag Myerscough

96

Environmental Design From the Intuitive to the Parametric

Patrick Bellew

104

A Symbiotic Relationship

Reminiscences of the Family

Joe Morris

112

The New Establishment

Politics and Performance

Frances Anderton

118

From Another Perspective

Old Buildings, New Architecture

Richard Griffiths Architects

Neil Spiller

128

```
AHMM, Soho Place,
London, due for completion 2022
```

Contributors

134

3

Editorial Offices
John Wiley & Sons
9600 Garsington Road
Oxford
OX4 2DQ

T +44 (0)1865 776 868

Editor
Neil Spiller

Managing Editor
Caroline Ellerby
Caroline Ellerby Publishing

Freelance Contributing Editor
Abigail Grater

Publisher
Todd Green

Art Direction + Design
CHK Design:
Christian Küsters
Barbara Nassisi

Production Editor
Elizabeth Gongde

Prepress
Artmedia, London

Printed in the United Kingdom
by Hobbs the Printers Ltd

Front cover: AHMM,
Angel Building, Islington,
London, 2010.

Inside front cover: AHMM
Burntwood School,
Wandsworth, London,
2014.

Page 1: AHMM, Yellow
Building, Kensington and
Chelsea, London, 2008.
Photos by Tim Soar

02/2021

ⓓ ARCHITECTURAL DESIGN

March/April
2021

Profile No.
270

Disclaimer
The Publisher and Editors cannot be held responsible
for errors or any consequences arising from the use
of information contained in this journal; the views and
opinions expressed do not necessarily reflect those of
the Publisher and Editors, neither does the publication
of advertisements constitute any endorsement by
the Publisher and Editors of the products advertised.

Journal Customer Services
For ordering information,
claims and any enquiry
concerning your journal
subscription please go to
www.wileycustomerhelp
.com/ask or contact your
nearest office.

Americas
E: cs-journals@wiley.com
T: +1 877 762 2974

**Europe, Middle East
and Africa**
E: cs-journals@wiley.com
T: +44 (0)1865 778315

Asia Pacific
E: cs-journals@wiley.com
T: +65 6511 8000

Japan (for Japanese-
speaking support)
E: cs-japan@wiley.com
T: +65 6511 8010

Visit our Online Customer
Help available in 7 languages
at www.wileycustomerhelp
.com/ask

Print ISSN: 0003-8504
Online ISSN: 1554-2769

Prices are for six issues
and include postage and
handling charges. Individual-
rate subscriptions must be
paid by personal cheque or
credit card. Individual-rate
subscriptions may not be
resold or used as library
copies.

All prices are subject to
change without notice.

Identification Statement
Periodicals Postage paid
at Rahway, NJ 07065.
Air freight and mailing in
the USA by Mercury Media
Processing, 1850 Elizabeth
Avenue, Suite C, Rahway,
NJ 07065, USA.

USA Postmaster
Please send address changes
to *Architectural Design,*
John Wiley & Sons Inc.,
c/o The Sheridan Press,
PO Box 465, Hanover,
PA 17331, USA

Subscribe to ⓓ
ⓓ is published bimonthly
and is available to purchase
on both a subscription basis
and as individual volumes
at the following prices.

Prices
Individual copies:
£29.99 / US$45.00
Individual issues on
ⓓ App for iPad:
£9.99 / US$13.99
Mailing fees for print
may apply

Annual Subscription Rates
Student: £93 / US$147
print only
Personal: £146 / US$229
print and iPad access
Institutional: £346 / US$646
print or online
Institutional: £433 / US$808
combined print and online
6-issue subscription on
ⓓ App for iPad: £44.99 /
US$64.99

Professor Neil Spiller is Editor of △D, and Azrieli Visiting Critic (2020–21) at the Azrieli School of Architecture and Urbanism at Carleton University in Ottawa, Canada. He was previously Hawksmoor Chair of Architecture and Landscape and Deputy Pro Vice-Chancellor at the University of Greenwich, London. Prior to this he was Vice-Dean at the Bartlett School of Architecture, University College London (UCL). In 2002 he was the John and Magda McHale Fellow at the State University of New York (SUNY) in Buffalo. He has an international reputation as an architect, designer, artist, teacher, writer and polemicist.

He has a long association with △D, beginning in 1992 when he was one of a very few young architects asked to exhibit their work at the '△D Theory and Experimentation' events held at the Royal Institute of British Architects (RIBA) and Royal Academy of Arts in London, alongside Daniel Libeskind, Coop Himmelb(l)au and Lebbeus Woods. In 1995 he guest-edited (with Martin Pearce) △D *Architects in Cyberspace*, the seminal first edition of an established international journal to herald the impact of virtuality on architectural design. This was followed by △D *Architects in Cyberspace II* (1998) and △D *Reflexive Architecture* (2002). His interests also include all manner of emerging technology, particularly biotechnology and synthetic biology. In this vein he guest-edited (with Rachel Armstrong) △D *Protocell Architecture* (2011), another groundbreaking issue.

He is the founding director of the Advanced Virtual and Technological Architecture Research Group (AVATAR). Established in 2004, the group continues to push the boundaries of architectural design and discourse in the face of the impact of 21st-century technologies. Current preoccupations include augmented and mixed realities, technological singularity (nano-bio-info-cogno convergence), Surrealism and science fiction.

As a teacher of architects, he believes firmly that students must leave university with a thorough grounding in professional techniques and protocols to cope with the immediate demands of practice, but that education must also teach them the mental dexterity required for the changing future of their profession. This △D shows how this dexterity has evolved at AHMM in subsequent years of constructing their practice.

He is perhaps best known for his architectural designs and drawings. His 35-year career can be seen as a drawn cartography of how drawing and architectural speculation have changed over the last few decades. These changes and the subsequent reinvigoration of the architectural drawing were explored in his △D *Drawing Architecture* (2013). His architectural drawings have been exhibited and published all over the world, and are in many international collections.

He is the author of numerous books on the education of architects, the visionary tradition in architecture, and architecture and technology. His two most recent books are *Architecture and Surrealism: A Blistering Romance* (Thames & Hudson, 2016) and *How to Thrive at Architecture School: A Student Guide* (RIBA Publishing, 2020). He is an active supporter of students and young architects, frequently publishing their work in this and other publications. △D

Urban Artefacts

Developing the Delightful City

AHMM,
Poolhouse,
Wiltshire, England,
1994

above: The interior of the
Poolhouse has a quiet, sparse
architectural simplicity, at once
functional, happy and delightful.

right: As the first project of the
newly inaugurated AHMM,
the Poolhouse gave them the
opportunity to display and
expand their architectural
lexicon in creating a highly
choreographed, small and
pleasing building.

AHMM,
Battleship Building,
Westminster, London,
2001

opposite top: The Battleship
Building is an instantly
recognisable landmark that
brightens up the often-drab
approach to Central London
along the M4 motorway.
AHMM's refurbishment
gave it a new lease of life
as a headquarters for the
Monsoon group.

AHMM,
Jubilee
Primary School,
Lambeth, London,
2002

opposite bottom: The school
was an experiment by the
client and architects to create
a 'super-school' that questions
and updates what a school
might be in terms of ambience,
layout and social integration.

I use the term architecture in a positive and pragmatic sense, as a creation inseparable from civilized life and the society in which it is manifested. By nature it is collective ... The contrast between particular and universal, between individual and collective, emerges from the city and from its construction, its architecture.
— Aldo Rossi, 1982[1]

This issue of ⟁ is conceived as an in-depth investigation into a longstanding, successful architectural practice examined from numerous standpoints. It is not just about the buildings, which are manyfold, but the human relationships and collaborations that have made them. It is also about how Allford Hall Monaghan Morris (Simon Allford, Jonathan Hall, Paul Monaghan and Peter Morris) have designed and constructed their practice over the years, from their beginnings as students to becoming international creators of large urban set-pieces and architects of some of the UK's most recognisable buildings, as well as rejuvenators of some of its cherished iconic places. Coupled with a willingness to use creative, lateral thought to find architectural and urban solutions, this has made AHMM one of the country's premier practices, garnering many awards and much professional recognition in the process. The practice is headed by four equals, each working to their specialisms to create a well-rounded, slick business. Allford and Monaghan run design studios, Hall focuses on legal matters, finance and professional skills – all under Morris's overall leadership as Managing Director. To provide a wider perspective on the work, Hall and Morris run design reviews on each project.

A Toe in the Water
AHMM's first commission was, inauspiciously enough, for a poolhouse in Wiltshire (1994), with all four partners working on the project. It could have easily ended up suffering from the architects 'putting all their fruit in one basket', as Cedric Price put it.[2] Yet it became a most elegant addition to Allford's parents' house, having a well-developed sense of itself and a comely presence inspired by Victorian bathing machines, but definitely of its era – modern, delightful, with an internal Modernist purity. It was an instant hit with architectural journalists, particularly when illustrated by architectural photographer Dennis Gilbert's images, some of which have an almost Hockney-esque splash. They teeter on the fine line between the abstract and the representational, reminiscent of the best of Le Corbusier, Eileen Gray and others who followed. The scheme is a simple splicing of functions – pool and guesthouse.

Since the beginning, AHMM's work has been crisp and well detailed, as has the organisation of their practice. With reference to Henry Wooton's translation of the Vitruvian values of 'Commodity, Firmness and Delight', Cedric Price described how these were useful to him: 'Commodity is good housekeeping, money; Firmness is structure. The Delight factor might be dialogue. They've served me well ... because I can hang anything on them ... The dialogue involves people with the future and with the intention, ... that the future might be a bit better than the present.'[3] His interpretation of this maxim can equally be applied to AHMM's architectural philosophy.

In terms of Commodity (housekeeping and money), the founding directors state: 'We make money to make architecture, not architecture to make money.'[4] As well as designing architectonic structures, the practice is adept at evolving efficient structures of office management and team communication, and disseminating the lessons, techniques and processes they learn from the numerous jobs they work on. Sharing such information as a resource is crucial to their continued success. Delight is taken in this dialogue as much as it is in building the buildings.

Throughout their career, AHMM have also become expert at importing seemingly alien functions into existing buildings, rejuvenating them into a new lifetime of usefulness and urban delight; a prime example, relatively early in the practice's evolution, being the Battleship Building renovation beside London's Westway (2001).

This 𝔻 issue starts with an interview with AHMM's four founders, who talk about the genesis of the firm, its philosophy and its trajectory, some of their key moments, their involvement in teaching architecture and being taught themselves, plus their ideas of praxis. To further set the scene, Paul Finch describes AHMM's architectural genealogy in relation to post-Second World War London, illustrating the practice's continuity with previous successful postwar architectural firms, but also their differences. Peter Cook, former Chair of the Bartlett School of Architecture, University College London (UCL), fondly remembers the AHMM design unit there in the 1990s, their collective final-year design thesis and early student work, and their annual strategic and tasty intrepid lunches.

The Humanistic City
AHMM's approach as a practice is elucidated and articulated in Allford's contribution to this issue of 𝔻 (pp 38–45) – that the city can be transformed from the ordinary to the 'ExtraOrdinary'. This means always rethinking the fundamentals of what architects and urban designers have been taught and have accepted. They re-examine the form/function dialectic, loosening it to accept change and introducing dynamic mixed and blended programming. Above all, AHMM consider the public urban realm as the putty that holds the city together. In this respect, one is reminded of architect and urban theorist Camillo Sitte's book *The Art of Building Cities*, first published in Vienna in 1889.[5] Sitte was one of the most eloquent critics of mechanical planning. His ideal architect and city-planner was a person of taste and not a purely number-crunching, top-down urban dictator predicated on scientific expediency. True architecture and city planning, he postulated, should operate on a totally different level from that of technical issues. Sitte applied himself to the matter of public life in the city and explored the problem of whether in a modern metropolis the setting for it could still be scaled to the modern citizen.

To many, in Sitte's time, his search for rules that underlie the essential beauty of towns and cities of the past seemed to be nothing more than sentimental romanticism. As the 20th century progressed, the social, utopian, regulatory and engineering aspects of city planning seemed to have largely pushed out the progressive in planning and urban design. Consequently, today our cities have not engaged enough with Sitte's notion of public life, and the public realm is often sacrificed to commercial concentration. Urban design has become almost nonexistent in our contemporary cities. However, we are becoming more and more disillusioned with the ruthless, chaotic commercialism and the doctrinaire municipal uniformity that mark our 'new' conurbations. AHMM's preoccupation as students, and subsequent interest in the Nolli plan of Rome (1748) that mapped the city's public space, indicate a similar way of thinking to Sitte. Their contribution to the public life of the city, particularly London, and development of new, dynamic, diverse public spaces has been considerable as they continue to create sustainable, agreeable, delightful and yet commercially viable architectures that stitch together often-forgotten and derelict parts of cities. They reconcile taste with financial viability and give back to the city: 'As students we saw ourselves as steeped in the Modernist tradition and its inheritors, but we were critical and not beholden to it as a religious movement; we had seen that the best intentions of a brave new world designed by architects for architects had too often created the very opposite of a New Jerusalem!'[6]

There is still a concern for the Modernist social project and its aspiration to enhance the existence of the citizen, the pedestrian, the worker and the dweller. Isabel Allen's contribution (pp 46–53) charts AHMM's substantial history of housing projects and the evolution of their expertise in this respect.

Creative Collaboration in Many Sectors
The ability to secure numerous repeat commissions from clients and developers is a testament to the thoughtful and professional service that AHMM provide. Their success is also partly due to the loyal respect of many cross-disciplinary built environment professionals. Serial collaborator and client, developer Roger Zogolovitch (pp 82–7), implores us to sit at the dining table as he and Simon Allford make a couple of projects, the most recent in a long friendship and client/architect collaboration. Structural engineer Hanif Kara (pp 88–95) reflects on his considerable association with AHMM, including some of the buildings they have made together, and his teaching at Harvard with Simon Allford. Other collaborators also record their thoughts, histories and achievements working alongside AHMM. These include graphic designer Morag Myerscough (pp 96–103) who, over a substantial period of time, has brought colour to some of the practice's projects, giving them vivacity both internally and externally. Environmental engineer Patrick Bellew (pp 104–11) describes some of the innovative projects he has worked on with AHMM over the years, and architect Joe Morris (pp 112–17) tells his story from AHMM student through to collaborating with them nowadays. Collaboration and dialogue (Delight) manifests itself throughout this 𝔻 as it is the modus operandi of the firm in all its manifestations and locations.

AHMM have worked on numerous arts projects, a recent example being Liverpool's Royal Court (2018). The practice has a pre-eminence and expertise in education design. They have produced some of the most innovative school designs of the last 20 years, including the award-winning Westminster Academy (2007), Jubilee Primary School (2002) and Stirling Prize-winning Burntwood School (2014), all in London. They have worked with universities on halls of residence, for example Scape Greenwich at Ravensbourne University in London (2014) and the University of Amsterdam (2018). Ellis Woodman (pp 62–9) explores this particular trajectory using some prime examples.

AHMM,
Liverpool Royal Court
Theatre, Liverpool,
England,
2018

top: The Nolli plan did not just map
Rome's streets and outside open
spaces such as piazzas, it also recorded
interior spaces of public gathering.
A preoccupation with these types of
spaces continues to excite AHMM to
this day.

AHMM,
Scape Greenwich,
Ravensbourne University,
London,
2014

bottom: Scape provides student
accommodation, a ground-floor
multipurpose social space and individual
or group break-out learning spaces,
topped with a barrel-vaulted roof line.

The ability to secure
numerous repeat
commissions from
clients and developers
is a testament to
the thoughtful and
professional service
that AHMM provide

AHMM,
New Scotland Yard,
Westminster London,
2016

Here, New Scotland Yard as
seen from the south side of
the River Thames. It is a sturdy
building given finesse by
AHMM's sensitive additions.

AHMM,
New Scotland Yard,
London,
2016

New Scotland Yard, with its iconic and frequently televised entrance, is another example of AHMM's ability to breathe life into older, existing buildings.

The practice has also undertaken much speculation and research on the changing nature of office accommodation, and has built many fine examples at all scales of this use type that are flexible and responsive to the vicissitudes of the contemporary commercial landscape. Martyn Evans speculates, in a post-pandemic environment, what the 'new normal' in office design might be, and what AHMM could bring to the party.

Ten years or so ago AHMM established a now-thriving American outpost in Oklahoma City, which brings the lessons, skills and techniques they have learnt in the European context to the US, and particularly to OKC's architectural legacy. Jay Merrick (pp 70–81) takes us on a whistlestop tour. The view from the American side of the pond is further explored in Frances Anderton's perceptive piece (pp 118–27) about her relationship with Allford and Monaghan, and two very important current projects: Richmond House for the temporary relocation of the House of Commons whilst the Palace of Westminster, Charles Barry and Augustus Pugin's masterpiece and home to the Houses of Parliament, is being refurbished; and Soho Place, which as well as offices includes London's first newbuild West End theatre for 50 years, on a highly complex site. These two projects are the most recent of AHMM's institutional buildings, which also include New Scotland Yard (2016), the headquarters of London's Metropolitan Police.

As Italian Architect Aldo Rossi recognised: 'It is inconceivable to reduce the structure of urban artifacts to a problem of organizing some more or less important function. Precisely this serious distortion has impeded and in large measure continues to impede any real progress in the studies of the city.'[7] The final article of the issue, 'From Another Perspective' (pp 128–33), considers the history of Richard Griffiths Architects and the firm's work alongside AHMM, for example the rearticulation of the old Royal London Hospital within its Whitechapel context, which involved installing civic and community uses into spaces that were built for medical functions to convert it into Tower Hamlets Civic Centre. Here, new architecture can be made from old buildings, another speciality of these versatile architects.

AHMM have a long and continuing story, and it is impossible to record all of it in this publication. However, ⌀ hopes that it has provided some helpful vignettes into the construction of this very important practice. ⌀

Notes
1. Aldo Rossi, *The Architecture of the City*, Oppositions Books/MIT Press (Cambridge, MA and London), 1982, p 21.
2. Cedric Price, 'Introduction', in *Burning Whiteness, Plump Black Lines: the Projects of Spiller Farmer Architects,* vol 1, Spiller Farmer Publications (London), 1990, inside front cover.
3. Cedric Price, *Re: CP,* ed Hans Ulrich Obrist, Birkhäuser (Basel, Boston and Berlin), 2003, p 57.
4. AHMM, *The Founders Statement*, December 2018, unpaginated: www.ahmm.co.uk/assets/uploads/AHMM_The_Founders_Statement.pdf.
5. Camillo Sitte, *The Art of Building Cities: City Building According to Its Artistic Fundamental*s, Martino Fine Books (Eastford, CT), p 146. First published in Vienna in 1889.
6. Interview with the author, June 2020.
7. Aldo Rossi, *op cit*, p 47.

SETTING THE STAGE

Neil Spiller

DRESSING IT AND MAKING THE PROPS

AHMM Founders,
Old Street,
London,
2019

From left to right:
Simon Allford,
Jonathan Hall,
Paul Monaghan and
Peter Morris.

AHMM,
Soho Place,
London,
2020

Soho Place is a mixture of office/retail and a
five-storey, 350-seat theatre. Situated at the
nexus of Oxford Street and Tottenham Court
Road, it is an urban and structural jigsaw
above and below ground negotiating the
complex urban fabric and the underground
tube and Crossrail lines below.

Editor of **ᴗ Neil Spiller** interviews the four founders of **AHMM: Simon Allford, Jonathan Hall, Paul Monaghan and Peter Morris**. The discussion embraces topics that include the history of the firm, architectural education and above all their thoughts on architectural praxis and the pragmatic philosophies behind the practice and its success.

All the world's a stage,
And all the men and women merely players;
They have their exits and their entrances,
And one man in his time plays many parts
— William Shakespeare, *As You Like It*[1]

AHMM is a multinational architectural practice with offices in London and Bristol in the UK and Oklahoma in the US. They build all over the world and are one of the UK's most successful practices. The firm's founders are well-known figures in the profession in their own right and have contributed greatly to architectural professional culture, architectural education, mentoring of younger practices as well as building at scales from small to very big.

The story of AHMM begins in the mid-1980s at the Bartlett School of Architecture, University College London (UCL). The founders recall how their 5th-year tutor Jon Corpe 'taught us how to work together – by pursing the idea and creating the diagram of the building – whilst also working independently – the best ideas are common property to be developed and not owned by their author. At the same time David Dunster (Head of 5th year) taught us how to take risks. Collectively they taught us that everything – architecture, education, partnership – comes back to design in one form or another and, with it, the importance of taking individual responsibility.'

BEGINNINGS

A hugely catalytic, academic project cemented the four aspiring architects together, one that continues to resonate to this day. It was called The Fifth Man (1986). The four worked together as a team, eschewing the idea of the lone-genius architect-demagogue that students are often afflicted with. Teamwork, mutual respect and supportive negotiation were the watchwords of their collaboration. They describe The Fifth Man as being 'predicated on twin beliefs. First, it is in the field of everyday buildings rather than public building that modern architecture has failed the City. Second, that functional programme alone is not sufficient to generate an architecture.' A manifesto for The Fifth Man was also written and many of its key statements have been enshrined in the Founders' Statement that coincided with the move of the practice to an employee ownership trust (EOT) in 2017. It was also the source of the name of AHMM's publishing house.

Asked what gave them the idea to form an architectural office, they answer: 'No one thing, but five years of working together under our belts – at university, in practice and on competitions in our spare time – and having gained some recognition for winning a few of these, the growing sense that it was now or never. We were just qualified and in our mid- to late 20s so there was also unqualified optimism (you might call it necessary naivety), driven by blind faith, ignorance and

AHMM,
Paternoster Square location plan,
The Fifth Man, group final-year thesis,
Bartlett School of Architecture,
University College London (UCL),
1986

The germination of the AHMM ethos comes from this project,
particularly in relation to townscape and city building.
Absence of building is designed as much as the buildings,
deeply meshing itself into its contextual urban fabric.

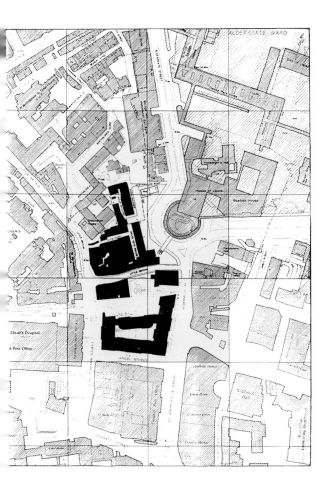

a belief in our own ability to operate as a team. We didn't know there was a recession coming, but in retrospect, a good time to start a practice.'

The fledgling AHMM was not immediately inundated with work. The early memories are of 'many long days with little to do, occasional short days with too much to do, having no money, having no clients, cold calling, local ads, very early computer games, inventing projects, being over-excited at the slimmest of leads, always remaining optimistic, the generosity and encouragement of fellow architects'. They describe themselves at the time as 'young but old enough to realise that clients were inevitably circumspect'. Also, they point out, 'it was not just about how long it took to get anyone to trust us with any substantial work, but also how little work there was around in any event. But exciting it was and hope sprang eternal that there might be something around the corner that would transform the practice's fortunes.'

During this time Allford and Monaghan coordinated an AHMM design unit teaching at the Bartlett and were part of Peter Cook's rejuvenation of the School. The School moved swiftly from a rather staid, old-fashioned Modernist approach to a much more gutsy, polemic and exploratory environment not afraid to experiment. 'There was a positive attitude to invention, originality and the power of drawings. We ran a unit for about 12 years and really got into our stride when we started to research the important everyday building typologies such as housing, offices, schools and shopping.' It was a formative experience: 'The work of the Unit in this period influenced our thinking and has since become the focus of the practice. At the Bartlett we relaxed some of the constraints of real-life practice to allow paper architecture to flourish – but we were always mindful that our unit must be a critique and not a mirror of practice. This focus on "generating the idea" has been central to how we think and create buildings.' Teaching also enabled them to learn how to direct design – how to 'shape and synthesise ideas into a project at close quarters and at arm's length. In that sense it created a model for our practice. We still teach now, as individuals and as a practice, as a vehicle for exploring themes and interests, and influencing how architects are taught. And to take ourselves outside of our own AHMM bubble.'

Doing It Their Way
The context, vicissitudes of fashion and precedents architects reference in their early professional years have a crucial impact on their subsequent work. AHMM have a mature attitude to these inputs in relation to their ongoing practice: 'Of course to some degree you can't help placing your own work in the light of what you see going on around you, and some of this work by others resonates with your own, some doesn't. But in the end, you are only responsible for your own work, and that's what we have spent 30 years focusing on. We have always been critically aware but also, wary of fashion, have let some of these fashions pass us by unaffected … Cedric Price and Will Alsop, in particular, showed how architecture could be rooted in humanity, yet challenging

and fun, and they remain a great influence on the practice.'

AHMM like to design from first principles, taking each project as a new beginning for the practice: each project is different, with its own joys and challenges. This examination of each decision in the cold light of day and not accepting received wisdom at face value can result in a sense of uneasiness in some. 'We wanted to discover and invent our own model – in practice as in design the iterative nature of refinement and uncertainty remain key to us. We have always held the view that individual responsibility for independent action is critical to making good architecture ever better – if everyone is comfortable with what we are doing, we must not be doing very much!'

The development of AHMM has been through a variety of stages of growth and has garnered many achievements. Some of the important ones are: 'All of the firsts: first published project; built project; new-build project (four elevations); open competition win; award; completed house / school / office / apartment block / gallery / bus station. But we waited a good five years – these years spent together with nothing helped to shape the relationships between us and form the foundation, so that when we grew we were ready for it.'

Changes With Time

Over the last three decades, being an architect has changed. The profession's role in the construction industry and its use and exploitation of digital technology have all seismically readjusted since AHMM was formed. Although they fully acknowledge that 'IT/technology has brought some efficiencies and enabled new means of representation, whether through drawings or models (physical and virtual)', the founders stress that 'in our work it remains a tool and not, in itself, a generator of design. The industry-wide step-change in productivity also brings challenges and the trick is not to be a slave to it. As individuals we may have been the last analogue generation of students but we have always embraced the new technologies available. We now rely more heavily on models and perspectives rather than plan, section and elevation. And we can see the immersive programmes such as VR allow the exploration of space and detail that were impossible when we first began. However they must all be used to drive the idea and not blur the focus. Having said all that, sketches are still important and can often be the most powerful tool.'

The nature of clients, their size and aspirations, have also changed radically during this time. AHMM have a formidable client list but each job is a new challenge and a learning process for both architect and client. 'We have made it our business to work with some very far-sighted clients and so, yes, their aspirations evolve from one project to the next, as do ours with them. Indeed we look to challenge our clients as a test of us both. Good clients are ambitious, want the best, push hard and are prepared to explore opportunities to push boundaries and accepted solutions – and are open to reasoned arguments and ideas if rationally presented in understandable terms. All clients are commercial clients in that they understand that a design that simply maximises area to cost is not the criteria for the long-term success of a building. In that sense no change. Ultimately clients want you to spend their money wisely and we respect that trust. By building confidence through long-term relationships we and our clients have become more sophisticated and adventurous – be it in terms of taking risks in construction, the assembly of materials or helping a high-carbon industry become a positive force in a low-carbon future. Transparency and the willingness to raise doubts and ask questions in the pursuit of clarity are key.'

AHMM,
Walsall Bus Station,
Walsall,
West Midlands,
2000

Walsall Bus Station is about reconciling the dynamics of cars, buses and people to create a civilised delight in using bus travel. It is characterised by its roof lights which let daylight deep into its plan and provide a sense of playful joy.

The guiding ethos of AHMM is a belief in the divine in the mundane and the ability of the everyday to fascinate and empower users and viewers of their buildings, as well as the ability of the building to be an enhancing catalyst in all aspects of life. 'On the most basic level we believe there is poetry and delight to be found in all buildings – be they the much-maligned office, school or factory.' Crucially, the firm's founders 'have never been interested in architecture as statement. We have always said that it is in the creation of the everyday, the background buildings that modern architecture has failed the city. That is why when there were two competitions advertised in Walsall (one for an art gallery, one for a bus station) in the early nineties we pursued and won the Bus Station.' As commissions have become larger and more complex, the firm has engaged in larger pieces of the urban fabric, rearticulating and stitching new architectural elements into the older, run-down or vacant to rejuvenate them into functioning and pleasurable city set pieces. 'We have sought projects that are complex and challenging and demand much of us and our clients. At Barking we kept the fragment of a building and looked to make a new series of five ordinary buildings: housing, hotel and small library, around a new public space. Ten years on we have done the same at Camden Lock except in this case alongside housing there are two market buildings, a school and three squares as well as a series of new routes woven between the early and mid-19th-century infrastructure of railway viaduct and canal. At the Bower and White Collar Factory, two separate but nearby projects commissioned by different clients at similar times, we have managed to build new, retain, extend and reinvent a dozen buildings that work together to create a new pedestrian and back land route, a little quarter of yard and alley that transforms not only our sites but the urban character of a previously fractured fragment of East London. The programme of live, work and play is the background programme of the city – the architecture pursues particular interests of ours, but the incidental city making is a beneficial side effect!'

AHMM,
Barking Central mixed-use urban quarter,
London,
2010

Barking Central is a piece of urban place-making that creates a colourful, convivial urban square, encouraging a deep sense of community, whilst also providing amenity for residents, workers and passers-by.

AHMM,
Hawley Wharf,
Camden Lock,
London,
2018

above: This project is another example of AHMM's aptitude for masterplanning and their thoughtful mixing of uses to regenerate and reconnect forgotten and run-down urban areas. Here there are 170 new affordable homes, an open market and a school, to name just a few of the scheme's elements.

AHMM,
White Collar Factory,
Old Street,
London,
2017

right: This set piece of multi-use urban realm is the result of an eight-year research programme with developers Derwent. The aims included minimising materials and energy but equally facilitating differing uses and the spatial flexibility required in these changing commercial times.

Enabling, Delight and Time

The firm has been supportive to fledgling, good, younger practices, some spawned from its own ranks, finding them opportunities to collaborate on larger projects. 'There's a strong tradition in the UK of one generation of practices spawning the next and, while that isn't quite our story, we have nonetheless benefitted from the generosity of others in our formative years, and have always looked to behave in a similar way ourselves. It's how practices are built. If you spread misery you will live in a miserable world! As a practice, supporting younger and more experienced staff is vital to all our development. As a practice we seek to pass on accumulated knowledge and experience.' Collaboration is key.

AHMM,
The Bower,
Old Street,
London,
2018

below: AHMM are also proficient in reusing and augmenting older buildings. The Bower is a rearticulation of a 1960s office block retuned to the functional and programmatic requirements of the 2020s (offices and retail) but also consolidates its context with new pedestrian links and vistas.

AHMM has a very committed, happy and loyal staff. Many of its Associate Directors have been working in the office for lengthy periods of time, a lot for a decade or two, and quite a few were also taught by AHMM at the Bartlett prior to this. 'As a practice being able to employ former students and then to draw from a wider global pool of talent has been crucial to what we do. Without talented and committed architects – with an interest in everything involved from design to construction – there can be no architecture. And we have always wanted to build and retain responsibility for our projects – though equally we are then very happy to let go and for them to be taken over by the theatre of everyday life.'

Time and timing are also crucial to AHMM, as they are in the theatre, and the theatrical analogy is useful in describing their philosophy and ideas on the transient habitation, use and function of their buildings and their architectonic elements over time. Their friendship with Cedric Price and their admiration of his notions of enabling, delight, expediency and of not seeing the architectural object as an obstacle have inculcated a great sense of optimism and a 'can-do' and 'nothing is impossible' attitude in the office. Price further augmented their interest in the differing metabolic rates of cities as well as buildings, their elements, their technologies and their dressings in the theatrical sense. 'We talk "theatre", "stage set" and "props". The "theatre" is the constant within the building (the items that are first to be constructed and last to be demolished), the structural system and the promenade of stairs and lifts and connectors (an architectural mirror of the street in the city). The "stage sets" are the mini architectures within that may have a life of five to 25 years (not unlike the façades that frame the streets in the city). The "props" are the architectural furniture that line and copy the architecture – the pieces that are moved and adapted all the time to allow the theatre of everyday life to happily exist.'

Since even before the practice was formed, every man and woman has played their many parts, some fleetingly, some for much longer on the stage that is AHMM and the theatre of everyday life that is their empowering environment. ⚿

This article is based on email correspondence conducted in June 2020.

Note
1. William Shakespeare, *As You Like It*, spoken by Jacques in Act II, Scene VII, line 139. Written and performed about 1598–1600 and first published in the First Folio of 1623.

Paul Finch

Continuity With a Difference

Rising to Prominence

Architectural journalist, publisher and founder of the World Architecture Festival **Paul Finch** charts the ebbs and flows of the post-Second World War London architectural scene and its genealogy. He shows where AHMM fits into this family tree, but also how their embracing of 'generalism' and 'good architecture' applied to the everyday has set them apart from some of their peers.

AHMM,
Burntwood School,
Wandsworth,
London,
2014

This design won the Stirling Prize, and represented thinking about school design that engaged the practice since its launch, combining inspirational design with prefabricated construction.

The rise to prominence of AHMM since 1989, in terms of both architectural and business achievement, has been extraordinary. It is a story of talent, ambition, hard work and a refusal to abandon the idea of general practice during a period when many identified specialisation as the only hope for the future of the profession.

In thinking about their place in the history of British architecture, one has to try to recall the pre-Second World War era when, by and large, British architectural practice tended to consist of relatively small practices (by today's standards), and generally bearing the name of the founding partners. Continuity of practice and name was not unknown, but was usually the result of son taking over practice from father, sometimes extending to a third generation.

Public and Private Practice

London practices came and went, with exceptions like Dick Sheppard/Sheppard Robson surviving into the post-1945 world. That world was one in which the proportion of employed architects in the public sector increased significantly. By the early 1970s, a majority of architects were working for local authorities, the civil service, health authorities and so on.

Private practices, and the way they were perceived, represented a form of cultural apartheid. The assumption was that 'good' architects either worked for a (by definition) socially virtuous public sector, or for private practices deriving their income by designing for the same public sector where it lacked the capacity to do everything itself. So schools, hospitals, university buildings and social housing represented the acceptable output for private practice.

By contrast, 'bad' architects were regarded as a lower form of practitioner, interested in money rather than a greater social purpose; the work of their practices involved offices, hotels, factories and shopping centres. They were described, in a sniffy if not sneering way, as 'commercial'. Even if their architectural quality was inarguable, for example in the case of Yorke Rosenberg Mardall, it was the educational and health buildings that counted rather than buildings for those 'commercial' clients.

For a long period, this crude demarcation of the profession had a malign effect. It would be reasonable to argue that it resulted in specialisation of the wrong sort, with a coterie of architects carrying out much of the office design work in the City of London, for example. None of them, in the opinion of the city's former chief planner Peter Rees, were very good, and he made it an ambition (achieved) to attract designers of greater quality to work in the Square Mile.

It is an irony that architects regarded as below the salt could produce work that would later be listed: notably Richard Seifert, whose work for the property developer Harry Hyams produced among other things the Centre Point tower in Central London (1966), now converted for private residential use. Another example, by a first-generation practice now scarcely

AHMM,
Adelaide Wharf,
Hackney, London,
2007

A good example of housing architecture combining with a social programme: in this instance, private buyers, renters of 'affordable' units and social housing tenants share the entrance, foyer, staircase and children's play area.

AHMM,
Barking Central mixed-use urban quarter,
London,
2010

The masterplan formed a key part of the local authority's regeneration of a neglected town centre. Public realm improvements and residential-led mixed use generated a striking scheme.

remembered, is the Vickers Tower on the Embankment west of the Palace of Westminster, by Ronald Ward & Partners (1963). Good office buildings, for example the Miesian Commercial Union tower in London (1969) by Gollins, Melvin, Ward, tended to be overlooked when it came to architectural awards. Other practices seem completely forgotten – for example, Arthur Swift & Partners – even though output was regular if unmemorable.

Succession Planning

Almost invariably, practices that survived the founding generation of partners changed their name or style. Yorke Rosenberg Mardall became YRM, eventually being purchased after a period as a public company by another set of initials, RMJM, formerly Robert Matthew, Johnson-Marshall & Partners; Gollins, Melvin, Ward turned into GMW. This could be thought of as 'first-generation syndrome', where survival meant change of brand or nomenclature, or both. The alternative was a quiet fading away, as has happened more recently with the fine practice of Ahrends, Burton & Koralek.

Reasons for the non-survival of practices after the death or retirement of founding partners were (and are) varied. Sometimes, as in the case of Lyons Israel Ellis – a practice that spawned architects as distinguished as

AHMM,
Kentish Town Health Centre,
London,
2008

The inspirational doctor client for this community facility in Camden worked with AHMM to produce an environment that would be a pleasure for staff and a breath of fresh air for a public more accustomed to welfare-state blandness.

James Stirling, James Gowan and Richard MacCormac – talented potential successors went off to form their own offices. In this particular case it happened with the encouragement of the host practice and its generous partners. A related issue was one of personal contact, the basis for so much procurement before the fiercely competitive era associated with Margaret Thatcher began (1979–90). As the contacts of the founding partners retired themselves, it was easy for practices simply to lose lines of work.

Opening the Market

Marketing was still more or less banned by the Royal Institute of British Architects (RIBA), strange though that may now seem. Practices could not advertise; they could not market themselves in any way that might be thought of as impugning the capabilities of other professionals. So how did practices get work? The witty former RIBA president Eric Lyons (himself founder of a one-generation practice) once referred to the way architects would socialise with potential clients on the golf course: 'We weren't allowed to solicit for business, but we could loiter with intent on the 19th!'[1]

The past is certainly another country in respect of the economic structures of British architecture. Fee competition was banned between 1834 and the mid-1970s, and the RIBA fee scales assumed that all architects were equally talented, that they could all turn their hand to anything, and that remuneration should reward that theoretical variety rather than the true cost of any particular activity. This, incidentally, explains the rise and rise of the architectural competition as a procurement method: if you were going to have to pay the same fee, this was a way to ensure you were paying for the talented.

By the time the four partners of AHMM were entering architecture school, in the early 1980s, much of the world described above was beginning to dissolve, if not disintegrate. Investigations by the Office of Fair Trading and the Monopolies Commission preceded Mrs Thatcher, but were certainly in the spirit of consumer ideology which claimed that more competition must by definition benefit the public – an ideology she enthusiastically embraced.

So the 1980s saw the introduction of 'compulsory competitive tendering' for public contracts, ending a century and a half in which tendering was reserved for contractors and suppliers, and had little to do with professional services. Architects found themselves in a tough market, having to fee bid aggressively to win work for the first time in their history.

Culturally, radical change was also in the air, typified by two architectural competitions: for the new Hongkong and Shanghai Bank Headquarters (won by Norman Foster with other competitors including YRM and GMW), opened in 1985, and the Lloyd's of London insurance headquarters won by Richard Rogers and completed in 1986. Even though these were customised buildings for user clients, they were commercial. From now on, the office market looked like fair game for new

AHMM,
Roeterseiland Campus,
University of Amsterdam,
2018

Won in competition, this complex part-retrofit, part-newbuild transformed both the university and its locality, recreating routes and vistas that previous development had compromised.

generations of architects who could no longer rely on the public sector for work, and indeed no long worked in the public sector themselves.

Symbolic of the changing world was a decision by Arup Associates, the architectural arm of the engineers Ove Arup & Partners, to work with a commercial developer (Stuart Lipton). They had never done so previously and had to confirm the decision to do such a thing at a main board meeting. When Margaret Thatcher ceremonially launched construction on the site in 1985, it was symbolically the start of a very different era.

Bucking Trends in Difficult Times

The world of competition, of looser professional codes and freer thinking about the role of architecture – in respect of any building type – was one that AHMM took to with alacrity. As students Allford, Hall, Monaghan and Morris worked on a combined final-year thesis project called 'The Fifth Man', a mixed-use project in the City of London, they nailed their architectural colours to the mast with the following: 'It is in the field of everyday building rather than public building that modern architecture has failed the city'.[2] So urbanism trumps object building, and ordinary buildings really matter.

Subsequently delivering on those ambitions, the early years were tough because they could scarcely have launched the practice at a worse time: the great late-1980s boom was coming to a close, work was drying up, there were four of them and they were paying relatively big rent on premises in trendy Charlotte Street in London's Soho. Would this first generation even survive their first decade, let alone create a successful long-term business?

They did, as we now know, but the smart offices had to go, cloth-cutting was the order of the day, and the usual short-term measures were put in place (loft conversions, local newspaper advertisements). However, the practice retained its belief in the virtues of generalism, that architectural skill could be brought to any programme, and thus the belief on the part of many British clients and funders, that you could not design a new building unless you had done six of them before, was there to be challenged.

A series of competition wins set the scene for what was to follow, in particular the international competition for a bus station in Walsall in the West Midlands. That was certainly an object building (how could it not be?), but the urban design approach was essential to winning the job. Buses, as a part of everyday life, as well as being the occasion for a public building, marked a melding of the ideas in that student thesis. In the decades that followed, the ordinary building type became something of a stock-in-trade for the practice: schools, housing (both private and public), health facilities and, yes, offices, which to our age are what factories were to the 19th and 20th centuries – at least before the COVID-19 crisis.

In delivering on both a social and architectural agenda, AHMM have also bucked other trends, or apparent trends, in the world of UK architecture.

AHMM,
Walsall Bus Station,
Walsall,
West Midlands,
2000

The modest town of Walsall achieved some architectural fame at the start of the 21st century, with an award-winning art gallery, contemporary pub and community swimming facility. AHMM's contribution was this international competition award-winner, the practice's first major win.

AHMM,
White Collar Factory,
Old Street, London,
2017

From the running track on the roof
to the public cafe in the entrance
foyer, the design created a 'universal
building' conceived to be adapted
for other uses as may be necessary
over time.

The ordinary building type became something of a stock-in-trade for the practice: schools, housing (both private and public), health facilities and, yes, offices

For one thing they have remained the committed generalists they started out as, declining to accept the defeatist proposition that practices needed to specialise or die, and that they had either to be small or large – anything in between would be squeezed out of existence. These views were reflected in the RIBA's 'Strategic Study of the Profession' report in 1995[3] after a crippling economic period for the profession.

Some awkward questions were raised by that report, including how a medium-sized practice was supposed to grow? A second concerned specialisation: it was demonstrably the case that the work of certain specialised practices was architecturally failing, even if it was competent in respect of rules and regulations specific to particular building types. Hence that coterie of City office designers.

Like all principled architects, AHMM flew the flag of good architecture being appropriate to any building type (NOT questions of style or dressing), and indeed that this would produce buildings which would be resilient over time. This was particularly the case in respect of workplace architecture, where the mantras of 1950s and 1960s developers about space, cost, floor-to-ceiling heights, floor loadings and so on were proving to be hopeless in respect of building longevity, flexibility, adaptability and, in more recent years, carbon responsibility.

In this respect, the headquarters building for Monsoon, completed in 2001, was an exemplar project since it redefined conventional ideas about workspace, combining multiple uses and/or possibilities in a generously engineered (by Hanif Kara) structure. The building spawned the phrase 'white collar factory', which became the formal name of AHMM's later edifice on Old Street roundabout in East London, for developer Derwent (2017). The ideas explored in Monsoon, and in the Stirling Prize-shortlisted Angel Building offices in Islington (2010), have been brought to full fruition: the 'universal building' may start life as an office, but could become almost anything else over time, designed for change without substantial alteration or demolition.

The notion of mixed-use urbanism has been a consistent theme in the work of the practice in recent years, a rejection of rigid planning zones introduced in the decades after the Second World War. The mix of uses within a building could in a sense parallel the mix of building types in its neighbourhood – London as it used to be.

AHMM have managed to buck trends in respect of size (they are now one of the country's biggest practices, with a total staff of 500), suggesting their approach to architecture has been fully justified. So how do they compare with those first-generation practices when it comes to extending the continuity of the office as and when the partners retire? They have avoided what in retrospect was the mistake made by YRM in becoming a public company under the chairmanship of David Allford (father of AHMM co-founder Simon). Architecture is an up-and-down business, probably not suitable for the

AHMM,
AEP Fitness Center/OKC Ballet,
Oklahoma City,
Oklahoma,
2015

Only the basement of a planned wine store (intended to house 25,000 bottles) was completed before AHMM was asked to create a new sports facility, now home to a ballet company.

Stock Exchange even when, as in YRM's case, it was a multidisciplinary operation.

Nor have the founding partners identified a small handful of people to whom they will sell their shares, the time-honoured way of doing things that involves complex tax procedures and at worst places intolerable financial burdens on the successors (who have to borrow the money to buy themselves into the company). Nor has the extreme option been chosen: that of assuming things will wind down, fading away after the first few decades of success.

Instead, they have chosen to create an employee ownership trust (EOT), which transfers ownership of the practice to its very substantial workforce. It provides incentives for good designers to remain rather than setting out on their own, laying the foundations for the long-term survival of the practice as the founders, currently still very actively involved, depart the stage.

Practice today is a more complex matter than 50 years ago (with technology transforming the way design is generated), with concerns about gender, ethnic and sexual diversity, and the increasing requirements placed on employers to act as a combination of mentor, agony aunt and ethical exemplar. Other changed concerns relate to contract forms, client relationships and – not least – fee levels.

Again, AHMM have bucked the trend by declining to take part in a race to the bottom on fees, instead preferring to charge more than many competitors in return for first-class service that helps guarantee repeat commissions, plus design thinking that creates demonstrable value at the front end of the process rather than relying on the modest fees chargeable for working drawings.

This is an optimistic model about how practices might prosper in the 21st century because it assumes that enough clients will be more interested in value and service than the cost of fees, but it is optimism grounded in experience rather than theory. A strategic study of the profession today might take this AHMM model as a desirable norm.

There are enough lines of continuity in the world of professional practice to see clear connections between AHMM and their predecessors, but enough differences to make their story a revealing one. The practice has placed client and place at the heart of what it does, rather than adopting the lofty yesteryear attitude that clients are a necessary nuisance, philistines to be educated in the ways of the mother of the arts. This has been a necessary and welcome change. ◮

Notes
1. Eric Lyons in conversation with the author, 1975.
2. AHMM, 'The Fifth Man', unpublished written thesis to support design work, Bartlett School of Architecture, University College London (UCL), 1986.
3. RIBA, 'Strategic Study of the Profession' report, RIBA Publishing (London), 1995.

Peter Cook

Very Much an

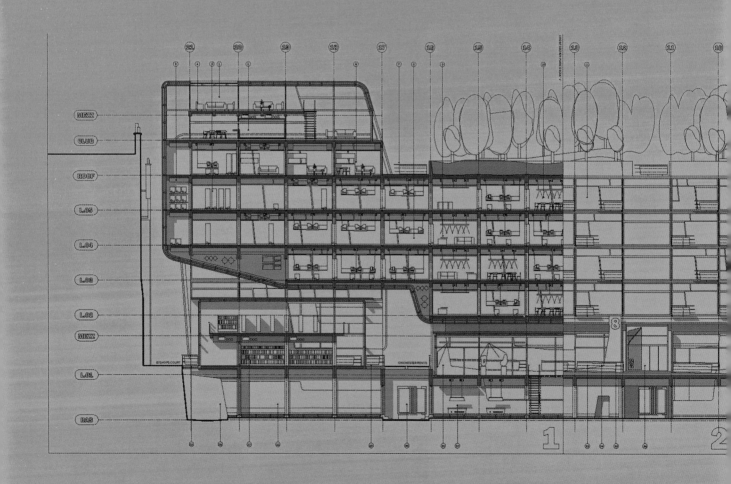

English Story

Philip Turner,
efficienCity,
Bartlett School of Architecture,
University College London (UCL),
2001

The multi-programme proposal for a site at the junction of the City
of Westminster, City of London and London Borough of Camden,
'efficienCity' is a new density model of 300 per cent net-to-gross work/
home/play. Uses change and spaces are shared over the daily cycle,
making a 'swing building' to address the alternate policy ambitions of
the three neighbouring boroughs.

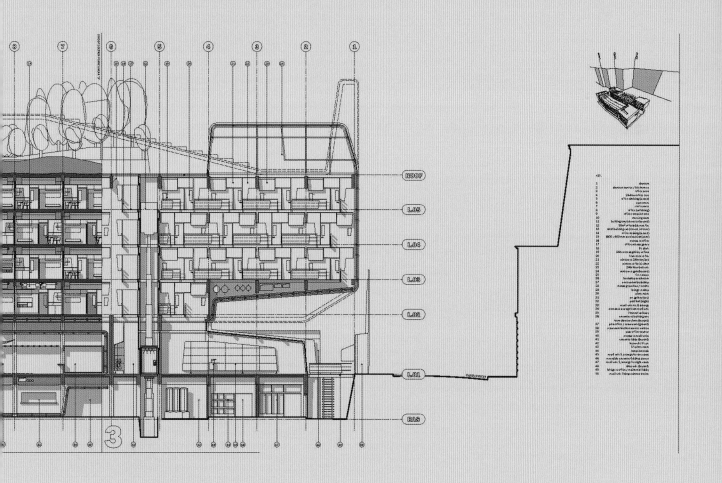

Archigram founder member and co-founder of CRAB Studio **Peter Cook** remembers early soirées at architectural theorist and historian Reyner Banham's house, coming across first David Allford and seeing the early flowerings of his son Simon Allford and Paul Monaghan as teachers and architects, and their subsequent professional rise during his tenure as Chairman at the Bartlett School of Architecture, University College London.

Before AHMM existed there was another admirable London practice that was highly respected, sometimes imitated, and intriguing by way of its ability to come up with building after building that was 'really rather good', but not shocking or quirky. Founded in the early 1940s, it was called YRM: standing for Yorke, Rosenberg and Mardall. The original three partners were respectively FRS Yorke (very English), Eugene Rosenberg (Czech Jew) and Cyril Mardall (Finnish) – a combination that pushed some of the Modernist ethics more forcibly than most of the polite English were able to do. Yet it was their protégées who made it their business to engage with the more progressive corner of the London scene.

Milieu and Schooling

So as I entered the Architectural Association (AA) School of Architecture in London in 1958, in from the provinces, I kept asking people: 'Who is that guy in a white shirt and a suit who has the likes of Peter Smithson or James Gowan taking notice of him on juries?' It was one of those protégés: a certain David Allford who, though originally from Sheffield in South Yorkshire in England, was (as I got to know him) clearly inspired by Eugene Rosenberg – his European-ness, his collecting of paintings, his crisp detailing, his robust style as an individual. Living nearby to me in Swiss Cottage and observable as one of the 'regulars' at Mary and Peter (Reyner) Banham's Friday nights, it all began to slot in. This affable (and very bright) man was assiduously collecting art – but English art and fighting the good Modernist fight, albeit with some Brutalism creeping in.

Now somewhere there were some Allford kids knocking around. Maybe by the time I really got to know him they were already up at university. Intriguingly, Simon first went to Sheffield, his dad's old school. I remember David almost apologetically saying that it was 'the boy's choice' to then move on, in the mid-1980s, to the Bartlett at University College London (UCL). This was in the company of Alvin Boyarsky, Chairman of the AA, who was one of his closest friends and undoubtedly Allford senior was a key link between Banham, Boyarsky and Cedric Price: respected by all as simultaneously a wit and a sage. Many times Alvin would seek Allford's guidance in tricky situations. Many times Cedric would confide in him. The fight for the AA's survival owes much to this advice. Yet, so the story goes, the young Simon did not like the feel of this elite school. Maybe the Bartlett was seen as more straightforward? Maybe, too, the fact that his friend Paul Monaghan was making the same move from Sheffield was a factor? Maybe, too, was the need to define his own trajectory, to avoid that cloying agreeableness of being the son of a well-networked parent?

I have often pondered on what Simon and Paul, the defining designer partners of AHMM, would have turned out like had they been at the AA in the 1980s? Would their architecture have been formally looser? Would they have been more overtly arrogant? Would they have absorbed that veneer of cosmopolitanism and international network of friends and references that infects even the most British of AA graduates?

AHMM,
The Fifth Man,
group final-year thesis,
Bartlett School of Architecture,
University College London (UCL),
1986

It was at the Bartlett when the founding directors of
AHMM teamed up, two (Peter Morris and Jonathan
Hall) arriving from undergraduate studies at the
University of Bristol, and the other two (Simon Allford
and Paul Monaghan) from the University of Sheffield.

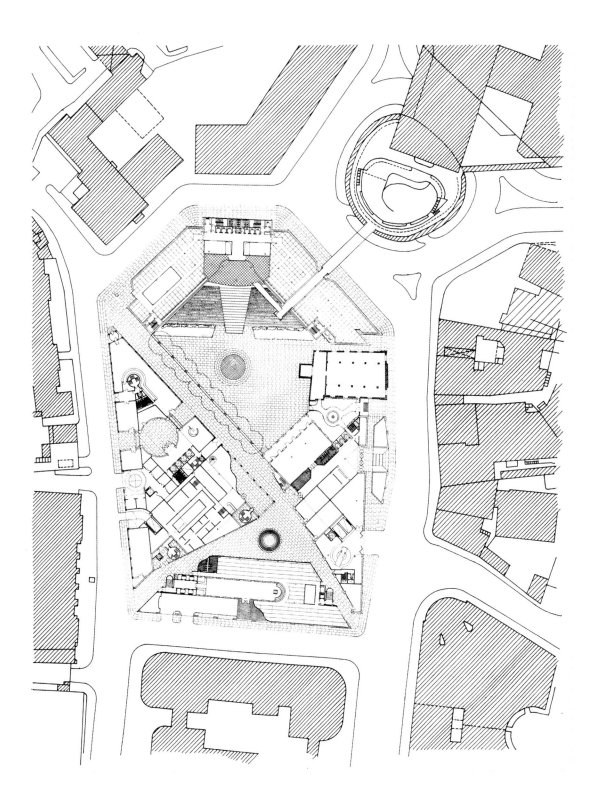

Simon Allford,
West Pier,
Brighton, England,
1987

Allford's competition-winning scheme while he was still a student is an elemental design the success of which rests on the composition of its parts. Each piece responds to waves, tide and wind to create a menu of spaces to bathe, sunbathe, watch and play.

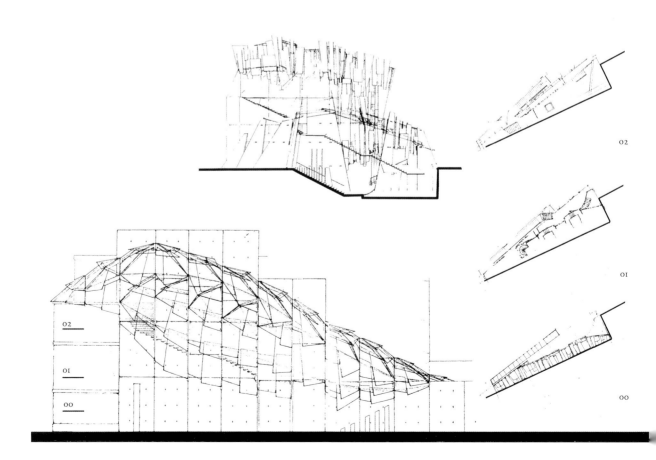

Unit Teaching

So when I arrived to Chair the Bartlett in 1991, the two of them were already teaching there – just about. Their student work was well known and Simon had won a competition for Brighton's West Pier (1987). Yet under the system of the day, they merely came in for an afternoon a week, operating within the brief and quite uncompromising direction of Christopher Woodward and unable to affect the rules of the game. Sniffing around to find out quite why the Bartlett at the time was so dreary, I did not necessarily have to clean everything out, and it was clear that these two were good guys. On the cusp. Ambitious. Raring to go. It was easy to see that they would rise to the challenge and develop a unit that could parallel the way they were developing their studio. It would be interesting to see how such a unit – referential to the real world, but not hampered by it – might bounce off the other, more arty, more esoteric or more experimental ones?

It was easy to see that they would rise to the challenge and develop a unit that could parallel the way they were developing their studio

Susie Le Good,
Restaurant,
Mercer Street, Covent Garden, London,
Bartlett School of Architecture,
University College London (UCL),
1992

A former student in AHMM'S unit at the Bartlett, Le Good is now an Associate Director of the practice. In this student project, the building clings to a blank party wall, with a variegated glazed envelope cascading over the linear floors. The dining experience moves along and up the spine wall with views through the glass, as if behind a waterfall.

There had been a slightly parallel situation at the AA when David Grey and then Rodrigo Pérez de Arce had units in the late 1970s and 1980s, where you were expected to do no-nonsense buildings in contrast to the rest. Yet here at the Bartlett I felt that Simon and Paul also had something to prove and something to say: they were straightforward, but sharp. Discovering the boundaries of the English situation and then persuading them forward. So sitting on their juries, I never felt that architecture was stuck in a pleased-with-itself straitjacket: more, there was a sense of urgency harnessed to the (reasonable?) objective of buildability. Over the years it became fascinating to see how students would pitch themselves towards certain goals, whether fame, notoriety or the quietest possible life, like dogs sniffing for a hole in a fence. It might be the girl (or boy) to be seen dating, or the pub to frequent, or here, the unit to choose.

After a while it was clear that several of the aspirants in Paul and Simon's unit admired them as role models and (quite reasonably) hoped that they could move upwards into the AHMM office – and this has certainly happened, for example in the cases of former students Susie Le Good, Philip Turner and Ceri Davies who are all now associate directors of the practice. Logical, economical and (in a great tradition) enabling the discussion of a project to be, in effect, a piece of shared research between office leader and student that might well slide into the office bloodstream. The two 'boys', as all of the Bartlett called them, were also quite canny as academic strategists.

Their lobbying for a student (or two) to get a distinction was an art form in itself, allied to the series of annual lunches (no expense spared) to which the two of them invited me. They were always good fun with a certain amount of useful plotting involved. I miss those lunches. In this connection, it is a sheer piece of education to watch the two of them 'work' a room. Give it, say, 150 people: they will each make as many as 20 feel as if they really matter, were great to see, had an interesting point to make – and then on. Close observation would reveal that they never overlapped, so that up to 40 people could be covered.

The Present

But what of the architecture? Nowadays AHMM is large and powerful, and has never become 'polite'. It can occasionally be a bit 'cold', a bit matter-of-fact, but quite often hits the spot.

So I will single out two particular cases, both in London. After having a thorough visit as a member of an awards panel, I was really impressed by the intelligence of the work. One was the block of apartments and work spaces at Adelaide Wharf in Hackney (2007), which has wonderful, really useable balconies. Indeed, they are not too nervous to rather often do good balconies. The other is the Angel

Logical, economical and (in a great tradition) enabling the discussion of a project to be, in effect, a piece of shared research between office leader and student that might well slide into the office bloodstream

Ceri Davies,
Urban Consumption restaurant and clubhouse,
Covent Garden, London,
Bartlett School of Architecture,
University College London (UCL),
1992

A private clubhouse that places the theatrics of utility and movement at its centre. An inverted cone, containing cloak- and washrooms, suspends weightily from the roof; a contrasting lightweight staircase circulating its form.

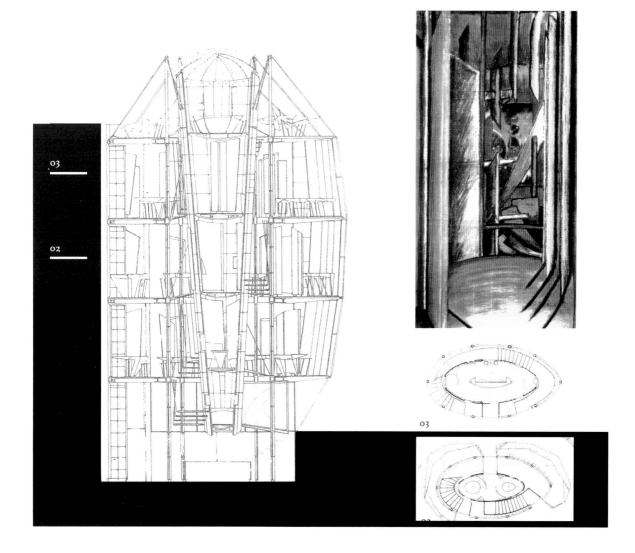

03

02

03

Building in Islington (2010) where the reconstitution of an office block eschews the temptation to make it all bricky and mushy and, again, combines many, many clever devices to create a superbly civilised environment and a great lobby. In both cases one came away thinking: this is the level at which English architecture should be – but isn't.

Yet the most intriguing project remains Burntwood School in Wandsworth, London (2014), for the 'boys' have finally come to terms with 'modelling' and beaten many old muddler-modellers at their own game.
In some ways I was reminded of Howell Killick Partridge & Amis (HKPA) of the 1960s – heroes of mine at the time. The facets work well with the English light, they create identity without exaggerated incident. (Their rival must now be Jeanne Gang, who is also great with facets.) But look at the corners, simultaneously considered and deft. Just the right touch. It is a very mature and satisfying building and yet it pushes the game forward – as they did with their students.

Underneath the apparently brisk and business-like 'face' of Simon is a sentimentalist – carrying on the close support and friendship with Cedric Price through to the end. Underneath the apparently softer and more discursive face of Paul is a fierce determination.

They are attracted to fun and games: Paul's wife, Alicia, was one of the most hilarious (in the best way) of students in my early days at the Bartlett. Another of their circle is Morag Myerscough whose exotic graphics – though very English – have contributed to several of their buildings (see pp 96–103 of this issue).

So as I came in I was describing an office that was highly respected, coming up with building after building that was 'really rather good' – and that's pretty OK. ⌂

AHMM,
Burntwood School,
Wandsworth, London,
2014

AHMM's rejuvenation of this mid-20th-century school carved out spaces for 21st- century teaching practices so very different to when the school was originally designed. The scheme won the coveted Stirling Prize in 2015.

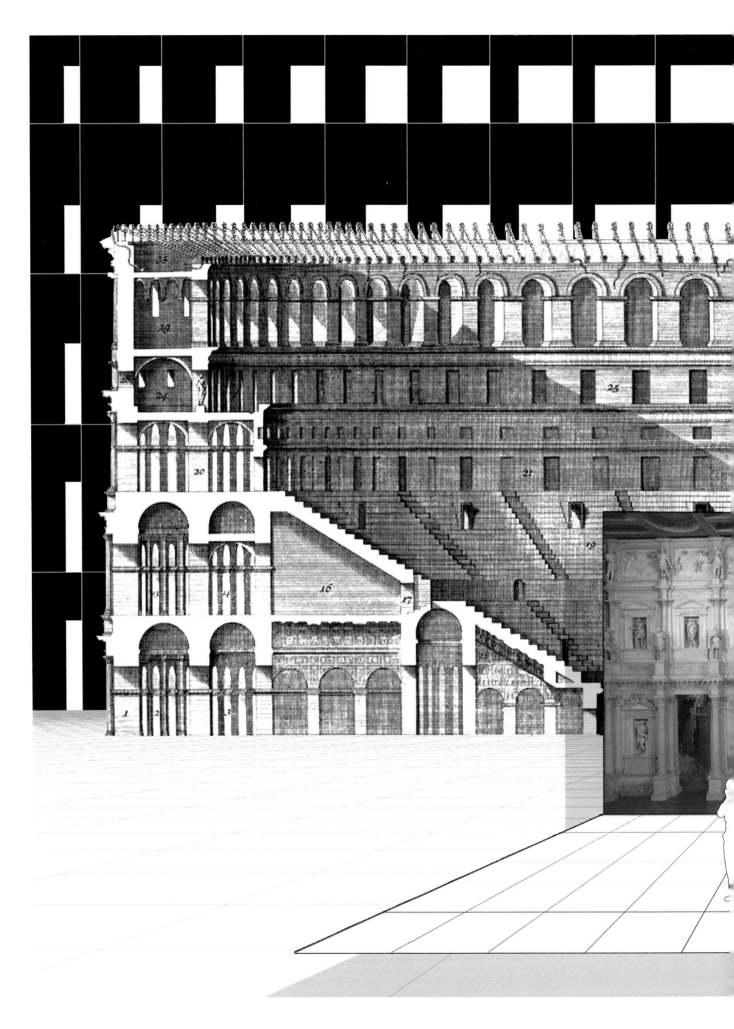

Simon Allford

THE EXTRA ORDINARY

Some Thoughts on Architecture and the Theatre of Everyday Life

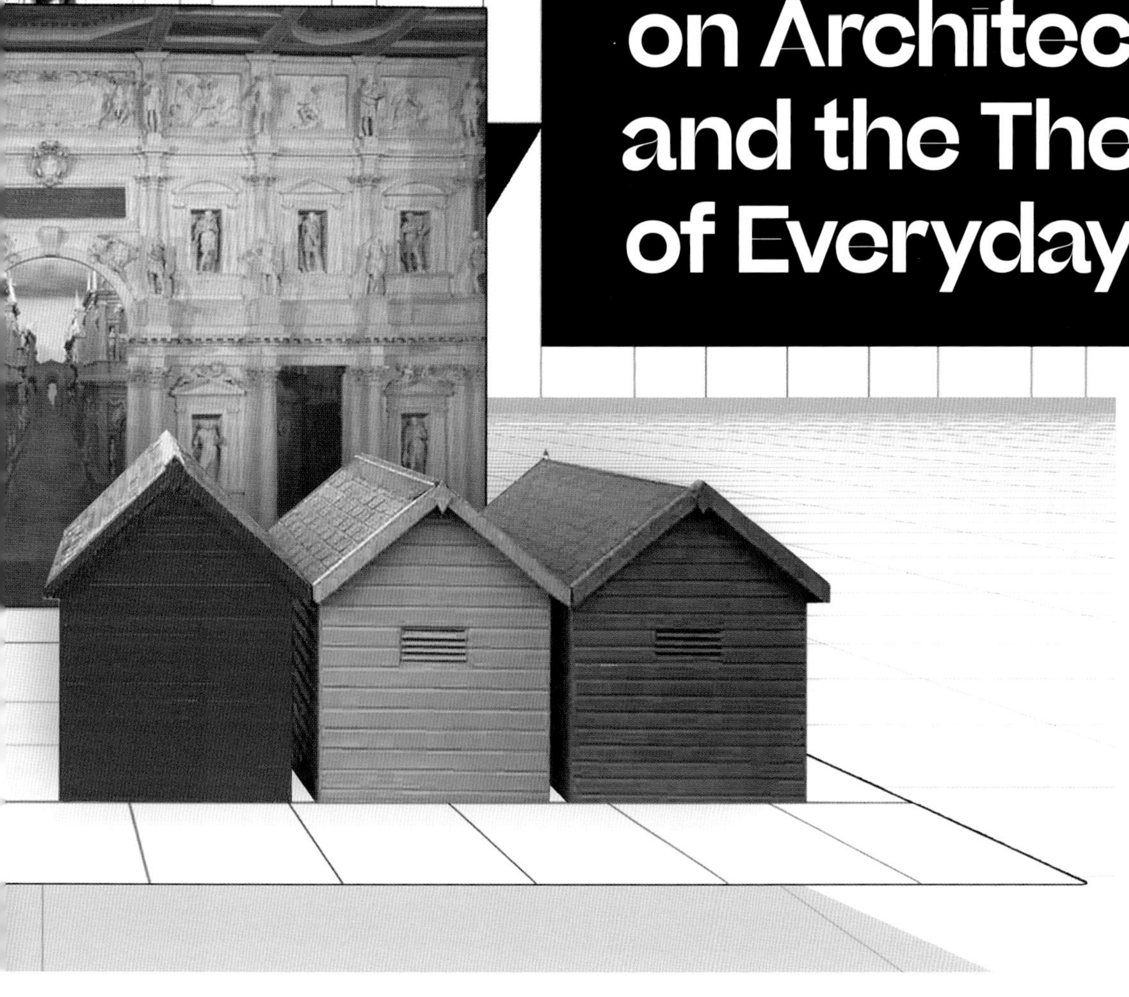

AHMM,
Theatre, Stage Set
and Props,
2014

The architectural brief for ExtraOrdinary buildings required by the Universal Use Class Order – as imagined by AHMM. Different elements of buildings have differing lifetimes: some are short-term and transient, others are long-term and more permanent. The analogy can be drawn between buildings and the costumes, backdrops and infrastructure of theatrical performances.

Writing on behalf of AHMM, **Simon Allford** describes the founding directors' catalytic joint project, the Fifth Man, developed in their final year at university: its insights, the personalities that influenced it and how, over 30 years later, its dictums are still a guiding light in their contemporary practice as they explore the idea of how the ordinary can become ExtraOrdinary architecture.

Ludwig Mies van der Rohe,
Seagram Building,
New York,
1958

The 38-storey Seagram Building was intended as a landmark head-quarters for the Seagram distillery company. They needed only the first six floors of the building, the remainder being designed speculatively for other commercial tenants who in effect subsidised the landmark.

Ludwig Mies van der Rohe declared: 'I don't want to be interesting. I just want to be good.'[1]

Our Professor David Dunster once said of our joint final-year thesis project The Fifth Man in 1986: 'It's boring – which is good; but unfortunately it's not boring enough!'

So boring can be good. Or put another way, ordinary buildings are good. They are fundamental to successful urbanity; and the particular qualities of very good ordinary buildings identify them as ExtraOrdinary.

The modern vernacular as pioneered by Mies is, in his hands ExtraOrdinary. The Seagram Building in New York (1958) is the endlessly copied but never bettered model of an ancient idea of enclosure formed by frame and infill, a universal space designed to be appropriated by programmes yet to emerge. But architecture must exist: as Mies wryly observed of each subtly different container, 'of course we did it that way as we best liked the way it looked'.[2]

The Bradbury Building in Los Angeles (1893), designed by Sumner Hunt and George Wyman, offers an alternative idea of the container. Behind the modest sandstone exterior is an exuberant galleried court, a theatrical promenade celebrated in more than 20 films, including Ridley Scott's 1982 dystopian *Blade Runner*. So there is no single way.

ExtraOrdinary buildings must withstand change. Giuseppe Terragni's Casa del Fascio, built in 1936 in the Italian city of Como, was renamed the Casa del Popolo following a post-war ideological switch. It remains revered regardless of the politics of the commission. Thus, a building is simply bad, good or, better still, ExtraOrdinary.

ExtraOrdinary buildings are memorable because they define urban space without and within. They explore the tension between the generic and the specific, and are neither restrictive of use nor defined by it. The identity of the author, the architect, the owner – or any mixture of these – is not always evident. Yet their specific qualities engage and challenge those who perceive and use them.

It was once anticipated that the rise of the virtual would de-structure and destabilise the city. That the internet would free us from urban life. But people continue to flood to cities in ever greater numbers. Why? Because cities act as social condensers and places of chance encounter, exchange and change. (Our small office was for a brief period on Alfred Place, roughly opposite Cedric Price's office; his greeting note stressed the import of the 'non-electronic network'.) So buildings are significant only in that they help define the character of the streets and suggest the culture of their time. Inevitably they come and they go. But the city itself shapes us. We commute to communicate and gather together. At the time of writing, COVID-19 is the current, next test of London the attractor – we expect it to pass!

The city is defined through numerous lenses: as a network, as a cluster of cultures, activities, people, businesses, and as a reflection of the governance of visible and invisible systems. But also by its physical infrastructure. Which begs the question why architects – who like to think they are creating cities – do not seek an involvement in the initiation of all forms of ambitious infrastructure projects? There are now so-called 'architects' of so many things: but why are so few of them actually architects?

Urban Collective Memory

Cities are also places of collective memory. So buildings as architecture inevitably both reference past activities whilst accommodating those of the present and the future. Even when building anew we are building on history. So, running a parallel path to the idea of the universal programme of use is the history of activity informing architecture and place. In the early 20th century, Shoreditch in East London was a centre for furniture-making. The activity is now long gone, but a century on it continues to define Shoreditch. Use dictated the size and scale of the streets and buildings, meaning that the legacy of the activity is embedded in the nature of the place. A potentially contrary idea therefore emerges: that use defines cities and thus how we should think about them. And if cities define how we think about architecture, then use remains important to us.

Intriguingly some factories designed for the pursuit of monotonous Fordist activity during the 20th century now readily serve as houses of creativity. The Tea Building in Shoreditch (2004) is a factory building being continuously redefined and reinvented. AHMM's design strategy there – robust and straightforward – has focused on the provision of inherently flexible unit sizes and configurations to attract a diverse mix of tenants. At Television Centre at White City (2018), AHMM retained and upgraded three studios for the British Broadcasting Corporation (BBC) but re-engineered the bulk of the outmoded (later and meaner and listed) offices to create apartments, whilst delivering a new container – that defines a new public space – for use as offices and a club (at least that is the programme for now). So, as the architects for these projects, AHMM do nothing more than enable new suites of activities to emerge. This 'non-plan' idea resists the creepy notion that we curate communities. Instead we allow them to curate themselves. Both projects challenge common orthodoxies of 21st-century technological progress. Let activity occur!

City Patterns of Use

Representation of patterns of use in cities defines how we read them and then what they become. Yet the city plan fails to show the activity of the sectional city. *London Night and Day* (1951), illustrated by English cartoonist and architectural historian Osbert Lancaster, offers a far more informative description of the city than either. As proclaimed on its cover, it is 'a guide to where the other books don't take you' that leads the reader around the lesser-known sights of 1950s London. Organised by the hour, it reveals city life changing over time. A reminder that just as we are drawn to cities by uncertain possibilities, so our architecture must construct possibilities for life beyond that of the current activity.

Regulations and overriding patterns of accepted logic are but the lowest common denominator to which we defer to our detriment. We measure buildings, and frequently, using a multitude of tools, but none of them

Cover of *London Night and Day*, 1951

Illustrated by Osbert Lancaster, the book offers a far more engaging description of the city than many maps, plans and sections of the period. As 'a guide to where the other books don't take you', it leads the reader around the lesser-known sights of 1950s London and is organised by the hour to reveal the changing life of the city.

measure pleasure offered over time. Which highlights
the absurdity of the city-wide regulation of specific
use-less Use Classes, as laid out in the Town
and Country Planning (Use Classes) Order 1987.
We need an alternative Universal Use Class Order.

Giambattista Nolli's map of Rome (1748) is
interesting because it represents the churches as
public space. Where are these public rooms in an
ecumenical 21st-century London? Would they be in
the pubs or clubs or schools or places of work – or
all of these? They certainly would not be in the silent
internet cafés. This loss of public rooms nurtures
the idea that we are witnessing the privatisation of
this public space – think of places like Broadgate
and King's Cross, in London. Whereas, in truth, large
expanses of public space have often been initiated
as private space. Both Broadgate and King's Cross
actually represent the opening up of previously
privatised spaces: beware the orthodoxies of the day!

Giambattista Nolli,
Map of Rome,
1748

Nolli's map concerns itself with the public space
of the city and the skein of urban connections that
choreograph public movement through the theatre
of everyday life there.

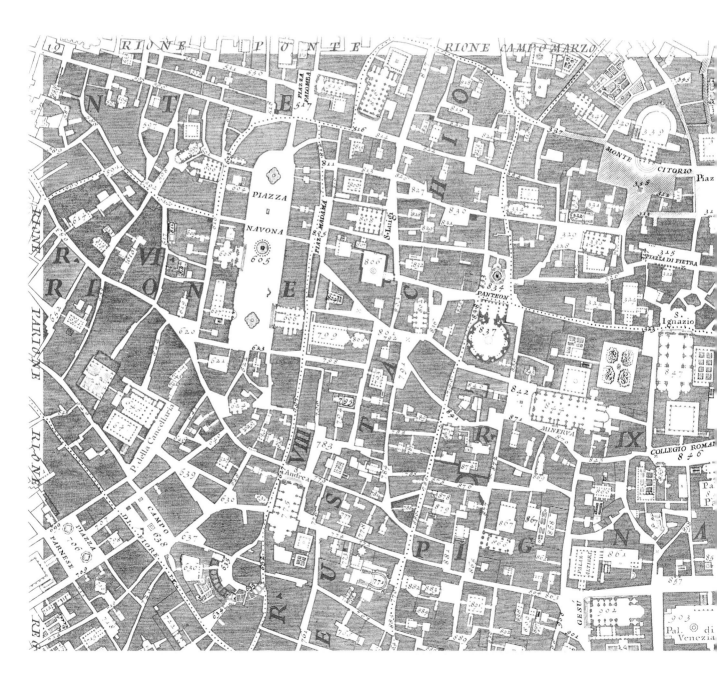

The caffeine culture of Shoreditch is but the latest reincarnation of the old gin palaces and older-still coffee houses: all disguising work as socialising and socialising as work

William Hogarth,
A Midnight Modern Conversation,
1733

A satirical representation of the drinking clubs that became popular in early 18th-century London. With increasing numbers of enfranchised professional gentlemen in the city, clubs became popular as a place for drinking and gambling, although many were also connected with the sporting, cultural or business interests of their members.

Passing fascination with buildings as objects (where the only real programme is to be an object) further promotes one of the great confusions of post-functionalist 21st-century architecture. Non-programmable (nor Instagramable) public space sets the scene but is not seen. The architecture on which the critics focus is but the defining backdrop to the public life. This facile pursuit of the new is naive: the public rooms of the new creative industries of 21st-century London would be very familiar to 18th-century painter, cartoonist and satirist William Hogarth and to 17th-century Member of Parliament and diarist Samuel Pepys. The caffeine culture of Shoreditch is but the latest reincarnation of the old gin palaces and older-still coffee houses: all disguising work as socialising and socialising as work. A successful model, endlessly re-described by each generation in its arrogant ignorance of the past.

The Fifth Man

The Fifth Man, our diploma project at the Bartlett School of Architecture, University College London (UCL), interrogated ideas of the city. We looked at the grid, the scale of the plot, and how plots related to the wider pattern. We discussed the efficiency of the city, and the new Big Bang city. We accepted the programme as secondary: use was of less import than idea of place. The Fifth Man was also a graphic play on Dutch painter Piet Mondrian's New York city *Broadway Boogie-Woogie* (1943): the life and jazz of *Broadgate Boogie-Woogie*. We noted that Manhattan, the great gridded city, works best where the grid breaks down – at the river edge and where Broadway cuts through. Contrary to urban myth, London is also a planned city (well actually lots of little plans), scrambled like in Cedric Price's vision of *The City as an Egg* (*c* 2001), where he conceptualised the evolution of cities as akin to ways of cooking an egg – the modern city being like a scrambled one. Its success is predicated on the fact that sites of collision exist at greater intensity and frequency than in the much denser Manhattan.

So if the city is all, and buildings are more important for what they define without than how they work within, why are we still obsessively making buildings? Partly because selfishly that is what we want to do, and luckily because that is what others want us to do for them. We can however only justify our social art if we make useful buildings – full of uses that change! AHMM have never been interested in the secret architectural design brief that some pursue. We are focused on architecture as infrastructure for activity.

But architectural infrastructure cannot be merely flexible and adaptable; it needs to be memorable and offer delight in many forms and ways. Otherwise architecture will not survive: no-one is engaged by an empty husk.

So what defines the infinitely flexible, adaptable and memorable? It starts with the idea of place within the wider address of the city. And then architecture must become present at that address: an idea of surface and skin (that goes beyond the nailing on of elevations!) that invites an emotional reaction from passers-by. Within this we construct the city in miniature, an architectural promenade. Architecture then exists throughout the journey from the street and through the vessel, passing by the stack of ever-changing uses within. Thus good buildings mirror the apparent freedom of the city. Then our architecture, like the city itself, becomes an accommodating backdrop to the ever-changing lives and needs of its inhabitants.

Places of work, play, living and learning may have become indistinguishable by activity but that does not mean that they need to become indistinguishable as architecture. For their architecture is then to be defined more by its place in the city than by its schedule of activities. So the essential urban building is flexible, memorable, and comfortably accommodates life in all its forms with a particular slant towards our species. A city within a city, defined by the quality of its volume, light, serviceability and attitude to technology and habitation. Delighting in its particular characteristic of Universal Use. This building of the future is here now and has been for a while – since the Renaissance, in fact. The architecture of the future exists in the Uffizi in Florence

AHMM,
The Fifth Man,
Bartlett School of Architecture,
University College London (UCL),
1986

Figure ground from AHMM's final-year thesis *The Fifth Man,* which interrogates ideas of the city. Looking at the scale of plots and how they relate to each other as part of a wider fabric, it discusses the efficiency of the planned, gridded city, and how this should be challenged to make creative cities – notably in considering programme as secondary, with the idea of place taking precedence over that of use.

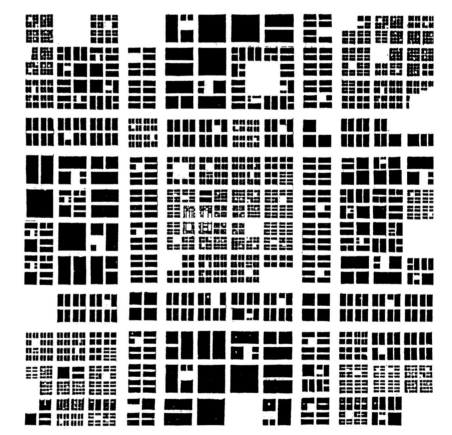

Cedric Price advised that architects should be interested less in the design of bridges, and more with how best to get to the other side

(established 1560). Not just an office for the Medicis. It was also their palace. A civic symbol and a working building. A place of work and a court. A home for noble families and their retinues. It is now an art gallery, but it always was. It defines a new place in the city. It is the perfect prototype and historical model of the tension between the generic and the specific. The Uffizi holds traces of all the previous incarnations of use, and is richer for it.

This idea of the Architecture of Universal Use addressing ideas of space, place and time is captured by us in the idea of the 'theatre' – a setting for everyday life, and an object in the city that should last for a hundred years and beyond. It is subject to forces of change which are acknowledged by 'stage sets' – buildings within a building that accommodate specific needs and that may last for five to 20 years. The changing needs of everyday life are then addressed by 'props' – architectural furniture that allows universal space to be endlessly reconfigured, accommodating both the generic needs of the city and the specific needs of the user.

This is the tripartite understanding which informs our pursuit of an architecture that is both endlessly reconfigurable and architecturally memorable. 'Theatre, stage set and props' is our architectural brief. This is about Slow Architecture, aware of but not shaped by contemporary fashions, and informed by the long history of architecture. Of generic and particular spaces accommodating differing needs at moments in time. Our architecture is about designing the *readymade* (for prescribed uses) that can then become *the bespoke* accommodating uses we cannot yet know.

Cedric Price advised that architects should be interested less in the design of bridges, and more with how best to get to the other side.[3] In the case of the ExtraOrdinary, the other side is the future we cannot see, but that we can accommodate. ⌂

This article is based on a lecture given by Simon Allford at the AHMM Spring Conference in 2014 and further developed in a lecture by the Founders at the Royal Institute of British Architects (RIBA), London, in December 2015.

Notes
1. Interview with architectural publisher John Peter, 1955: transcript in the John Peter Collection, Library of Congress, Washington, DC.
2. *Ibid*.
3. 12 design maxims written by Price for a 1972 article in *Pegasus*, a magazine published by Mobil Oil; reproduced in Gregory Vitiello (ed), *The Best of Pegasus*, Mobil Service Co, 1976.

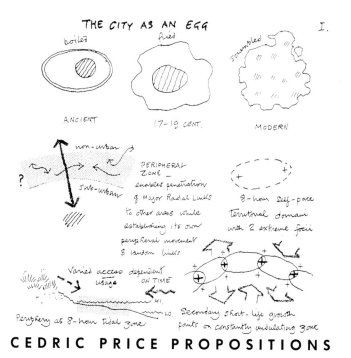

CEDRIC PRICE PROPOSITIONS

Cedric Price,
The City as an Egg,
c 2001

Cedric Price drew the city as an egg: boiled in ancient times and organised around a central 'yolk'; fried more haphazardly during the 17th to 19th centuries; and finally scrambled into the modern metropolis.

Isabel Allen

AHMM,
Adelaide Wharf,
Hackney,
London,
2007

Commissioned by First Base and English Partnerships,
Adelaide Wharf enshrined the principle of using
cost-savings from standardisation to cross-subsidise
generous outdoor space.

REIMAGINING THE HOME

Isabel Allen is Editorial Director of BEAM (Built Environment and Architecture Media). Here she describes how three decades of innovation – and an ongoing delight in the poetic possibilities of the home – make AHMM perfectly positioned to deliver a new kind of housing that responds to the practical and psychological challenges of these extraordinary times.

In *Towards a New Architecture*, published in 1923, Le Corbusier declared: 'The problem of the house is a problem of the epoch. The equilibrium of society today depends upon it. Architecture has for its first duty, in this period of renewal, that of bringing about a revision of values, a revision of the constituent elements of the house.'[1]

Every epoch has its problems, and ours are particularly acute. At the time of writing, we are facing the collective challenge of recovery from – or adjustment to – the COVID-19 pandemic: a period of renewal, a revision of values and, amongst many other issues, a revision of the constituent elements of the house.

For AHMM, a practice with a strong culture of innovation, this represents an unprecedented opportunity to review the way housing for current and future generations is delivered and designed. Having built some 10,000 homes – a figure that roughly equates to a dwelling a day for the three decades since the practice was formed – there is a rich repository of work to draw on.

This is a practice that views its output not as a collection of discrete projects but as a continuously evolving work in progress. Built ideas are seen as prototypes of refinement. This spirit of innovation and experimentation has been evident, in embryonic form, from the practice's earliest projects. Unbuilt ideas do not fall by the wayside but are set aside for the future.

Making the Readymade Bespoke

Two early projects – the tightly planned split-level Wiltshire Poolhouse, built in 1994, and a flat, for the architectural writer Jeremy Melvin in London's Waterloo, that shoehorned a mezzanine study into a tiny space – established AHMM as a practice with a propensity to think volumetrically rather than in plan, to layer multiple uses and interlocking spaces and to revel in the richness of mood and light and vista such variety affords.

AHMM,
Jeremy Melvin apartment,
Waterloo, London,
1995

This apartment for the architectural writer Jeremy Melvin signalled AHMM's skill in deploying multi-level interlocking volumes to create multiple layers, functions and moods.

AHMM,
Poolhouse,
Wiltshire,
1994

AHMM's spatial dexterity and predilection for multi-layered narratives can be traced back to the Poolhouse, a split-level building that combines swimming pool and living space and references precedents including the railway carriage, the barn and Queen Victoria's bathing machine.

The balconies at Raines Court reflect a determination to priorlise usablo external space despite budget and space constraints.

The UK's first Housing Corporation-funded modular housing scheme, Raines Court was an early example of the practice's ongoing project to 'make the readymade bespoke'.

But their interest in the poetic possibilities of the home is underpinned by the pragmatic streak that has propelled them from purveyors of bespoke one-off buildings to serious players in the housing debate – pioneers in the quest for quicker and more efficient ways of building at scale.

While other 'high-end' design practices favoured more conventional construction methods, AHMM executed a series of experimental projects including Raines Court (2003) and Adelaide Wharf (2007), both in Hackney, London, that explored the potential to build volume housing using modular construction, prefabrication and commercial construction techniques.

What lifts these projects from worthy experiments to notable architecture is what Simon Allford describes as the practice's interest in 'making the readymade bespoke'.[2] The interest in the replicability and efficiencies of programme is offset by a fascination with the moves that elevate a project from built experiment to architecture that enriches the city and allows its residents to thrive. The practice's enthusiasm for standardisation is fuelled by the knowledge that cost savings leave you wriggle room to spend cash where it counts. In this case, to temper high-density housing with balconies that are sufficiently generous to accommodate not just a sneaky cigarette, but a table and chairs, a meal, a catch-up with friends.

The company directors take particular delight in the fact that Adelaide Wharf – with its unusually generous 'yards in the sky' – was selected as the backdrop for BBC One's 2015 adaptation of Roald Dahl's *Esio Trot*, in which Dustin Hoffman and Dame Judi Dench play a retired bachelor and a widow who fall in love from the safety of their respective balconies. Whilst it might be stretching a point to read the plot as a prophetic insight into the challenges of dating in a socially distanced world, it takes on a new poignancy in a world when the elderly, in particular, are only gradually emerging from the experience of being deprived of social interaction and banished to their homes.

The Poetics of Space

The fundamental principle that housing, first and foremost, should allow humanity to flourish is enshrined and explored across all tenures and all budgets. In his essay 'Let This Be the Start of Something Big', written shortly before his death in 2018, the urbanist Hank Dittmar described AHMM's approach to 81–87 Weston Street, a high-end mansion block of eight interlocking apartments built in 2017 in the London Borough of Southwark's Bermondsey neighbourhood, as 'reminiscent of Elon Musk's strategy with Tesla to develop the technology in luxury cars before entering the mid-market.'[3]

The design is reminiscent of Adolf Loos's *Raumplan*, an approach developed on projects such as Villa Müller in Prague, completed in 1930, that views the home as a series of interconnected spaces with variations in function demarcated by changes in floor level and volume as opposed to walls and doors. A split-level arrangement allows each apartment to have two front doors on two different levels, offering the potential for one of the lower-floor bedrooms – and attendant bathroom – to be let out as a discrete unit with its own front door.

The similarities to Loos lie not just in the Weston Street building's spatial generosity and dexterity, but also in the richness and tactility of its material expression: timber linings and an abundance of joinery in walnut and oak suggest an overt

celebration of craftsmanship of which Loos would surely have approved. The combination of quirkiness and luxury makes it perhaps too easy to dismiss the project as a one-off; a classy little building for a privileged niche market. But it would be a mistake to overlook the applicability of the ideas it embodies and the lessons to be learnt.

At this end of the market, the existence of a spare front door – a secret entrance – translates as a neat conceit; an urbane indulgence that speaks of live-in nannies, house guests, louche lifestyles and French farce. It takes on a whole new level of importance in a world where economic hardship or the fear of disease impact on fundamental liberties. Where adult children cannot leave home. Where warring couples cannot afford to separate. Where households are compelled to nurse their sick – and manage the logistics of isolation – within the confines of their home. It is hard to underestimate the intrinsic value of an unfolding sequence of spaces that can accommodate – and perhaps engender – nuances in light and mood and prospect; that can facilitate myriad changes in activity, and modulate varying degrees of privacy and sociability, throughout the passage of the day.

In *The Poetics of Space*, published in 1957, Gaston Bachelard criticised the typical Parisian apartment for creating an environment where 'home has become mere horizontality'.[4] For Bachelard the Modernist preoccupation with rational planning and spatial uniformity fails to allow for the subtle gradations of intimacy that enrich domestic life. The house is – or at least should be – 'a body of images that give mankind proof or illusions of stability'.[5] Anomalies that subvert the clarity of the diagram – attics, basements, nooks and crannies, stairways, cupboards, wardrobes, drawers – are the spaces that ensure 'the house shelters day-dreaming, the house protects the dreamer, the house allows one to dream in peace'.[6] To reduce the home to its most basic functions is to make a world where 'intimate living flees'.[7] In Bachelard's terms, AHMM's instinct for variety and nuanced space is not simply architectural but inherently humane.

We have been forced into a new-found awareness of the twin horrors of enforced intimacy and enforced isolation. Polarities that once seemed a little *academic* – expansion and compression; enclosure and escape – have been thrown into sharp relief as we learn to live with the memory, and the fear, of effective house arrest. We have a collective new-found craving for space that, in the parlance of modern-day relationship counselling, is perhaps best expressed as breathing space.

Outdoor space – carefully considered, generous outdoor space – assumes an almost talismanic status in a world where everyone is grappling with the ever-present threat of enforced confinement. The rites and rituals of family life have assumed a new intensity. The familiar penances and privileges of domestic coexistence have been shot through with an explosive cocktail of economic uncertainty, enforced proximity and an unseasonal surfeit of illness, convalescence, mourning, grief and fear. The ideal home is one that meets our most primitive craving for security and shelter whilst simultaneously offering the possibility of escape.

We have been forced into a new-found awareness of the twin horrors of enforced intimacy and enforced isolation

AHMM,
Signal Townhouses,
Greenwich,
London,
2018

A development of 16 three-storey family townhouses, designed to fit into their immediate and future context within the quickly evolving Greenwich Peninsula landscape.

Anticipatory Architecture

As we spend more time working – and socialising – from home, it is also the place that defines our public self; the backdrop to Skype or Zoom or Instagram. Our understanding of the domestic realm has been turned on its head. The private has become public. The home has become the theatre of our entire existence – education, daycare, exercise, leisure, work. The simplest dwelling has been called into service as a highly complex building type, rendering it increasingly meaningless to think of housing as a standalone typology. In a parallel evolutionary development, changes in the way we work are challenging the notion of the office as a distinct building type, leading to an increasing focus on flexible mixed-use developments such as the White Collar Factory at Old Street Roundabout, London (2017), and the Television Centre at White City, London (2018).

AHMM,
White Collar Factory,
Old Street Roundabout,
London,
2017

below: This mixed-use development of apartments with offices, studios, incubator space, restaurants, rooftop running track and public space reflects a world where the distinction between professional, private and social life is increasingly blurred.

The practice's interest lies not in mixed use, per se, but more in what Cedric Price termed 'anticipatory architecture',[8] a 'loose-fit' approach to design that accepts and maximises the possibility of appropriation and change. AHMM's Founders' Statement, published in 2019 in a bid to articulate the practice's essential guiding principles on the occasion of the transfer of the majority shareholding to an employee ownership trust (EOT), formally enshrines the principle that 'the practice's work should be driven by a strategic approach to design that recognises that changes in circumstances and context, both during the design and during the life of the building, are inevitable.'[9]

Allford describes the practice's architecture as 'the theatre of life. The physical frame', adding: 'then there are the stage sets that are the temporary projects of life. Then there are the props.'[10] The trick is to differentiate between the three. To identify those elements of a building that have the greatest degree of permanence and to ensure that they are built both to endure and to accommodate change; to define the elements that can and should evolve and, finally, to allow the building users to make the space their own.

What is instructive about this way of conceptualising their projects is that it embraces the notion of flexibility without entertaining any excuse for the innocuous or bland. Theatre, stage sets and props are all highly evocative: triggers for memory and mood; the backdrop for storytelling, spectacle and delight. The 'constituent elements' of the house grow ever more complex, but its most valuable role remains unchanged: to nurture its residents, bring joy to their lives and allow for new narratives to unfold. Δ

AHMM,
Television Centre,
White City,
London,
2018

above: The reworking of 1950s and 1960s TV studios into apartments, offices, studios, restaurants, cinema, shops and hotel offers a blueprint both for breathing new life into outdated work space and anticipating future change.

Notes
1. Le Corbusier, *Towards a New Architecture: A Critical History*, Dover (London), 1986 republication of the work originally published by John Rodker (London) in 1931 as translated from the 13th French edition.
2. Simon Allford, *Extra Ordinary*, FifthMan (London), 2016, p 58.
3. Hank Dittmar, 'Let This Be the Start of Something Big', in Allford Hall Monaghan Morris / Solidspace, *Collected Volumes: The Story of 81–87 Weston Street*, FifthMan (London), 2018, p 19.
4. Gaston Bachelard, *The Poetics of Space*, Beacon Press (Boston, MA), 4th edition, 1994, p 27.
5. *Ibid*, p 17.
6. *Ibid*, p 6.
7. *Ibid*, p 27.
8. Cedric Price, *Anticipatory Architecture: Cedric Price Special Issue*, *The Architect's Journal*, 204 (8), 1996, pp 20–41.
9. Allford Hall Monaghan Morris, *The Founders' Statement*, FifthMan (London), 2019, p 15.
10. Simon Allford, 'Constructing the Idea: The Essential and the ExtraOrdinary', talk delivered at Harvard Graduate School of Design, 18 September 2017: https://www.youtube.com/watch?v=iPqye7mfERE.

As we spend more time working – and socialising – from home, it is also the place that defines our public self; the backdrop to Skype or Zoom or Instagram

A Passion to Repurpose

Flexibility for the Future

Martyn Evans is Creative Director of U+I, which specialises in complex, mixed-use, community-focused property development and regeneration projects. He looks at AHMM's engagement with office design, in particular their commercial, spatial reconfiguration, occupancy, newbuild, refurbishment and retrofitting expertise – a terrain within which they are renowned innovators.

AHMM,
New Scotland Yard,
London,
2016

AHMM's design for New Scotland Yard is a radical remodelling and extension of the Curtis Green Building, a 1930s edifice on the Thames Embankment, which was an earlier home of the Metropolitan Police Service. The core objectives of the brief were to create modern, flexible and efficient office environments.

AHMM,
Angel Building,
London,
2010

In North London a previously
unremarkable building occupied
by telecommunications company
BT became, by stripping back,
revealing its skeleton and
celebrating the core elements of its
structure, one of the most impactful
buildings in AHMM's portfolio.

While most of us working in the built environment are, at the time of writing, still sitting at our desks at home, itching for the starting gun to be fired that will signal the rush back to our offices and studios, the talk is of how the coronavirus pandemic will affect life in the future. The loudest debate is about how we will work. Will any of us ever go back to full-time working in an office? If we do, what will life be like there? Will any of us have our own desks? Will we even have desks at all? Will we do our head-down-at-a-desk work at home and on Zoom and come to the office simply to enjoy face-to-face intellectual engagement and social interaction with our colleagues? If so, how do our office environments need to be designed to facilitate this change?

Of course, none of these questions is new. Since the very first purpose-built offices, design thinking has developed to take account of changing taste, fast-moving technologies and academic research on workplace efficiency. Through all this, architects and developers have had to tread a very careful line in the arbitration of fast-changing trends and the time it takes to deliver an office building from first concept. It feels like an impossible task to ask an architect to design an effective modern office building for a workforce that will take occupation perhaps three years hence, once planning and building are complete. How are we possibly to imagine what that office should be like when we cannot predict with any certainty what is likely to happen within the next 12 months?

Developing Approaches

But, somehow, we have to find an answer. The key to AHMM's success in this regard is to have developed a series of approaches over time, resulting in a portfolio of some of the most successful office development projects ever built: an understanding that too prescriptive a house style will result in buildings that lose relevance; a passion for reuse that has been applied to existing edifices and the imagined future of those they create from scratch; a self-defined focus on designing 'everyday buildings in the city' that, through intelligent design and a professional methodology, can be made extraordinary.

At the heart of this is a sense of enquiry that does not rely on preconceptions but asks simply: how can we learn? It is this approach that led Simon Allford's thinking on the reuse and conversion of former industrial buildings to contemporary offices not simply by shoehorning a new use into an old shell, but by understanding why those original buildings were designed in the first place and adapting those principles of design for a new use. AHMM has developed a strategic approach to the practice's design which recognises that changes in circumstances and context, both during the design and during the life of their buildings, are inevitable.

In 2012 at the Old Vinyl Factory in Hayes, West London, property company U+I commissioned AHMM to consider the redesign of a collection of Wallis, Gilbert & Partners buildings built for EMI in the 1920s. This important group of structures had been mostly empty since the 1980s.

AHMM,
The Record Store, London,
2018

The Record Store at the Old Vinyl Factory in West London is a redevelopment of an original Wallis, Gilbert & Partners building from 1927 – a building where AHMM's White Collar Factory principles could be played out to maximum effect.

One building, The Record Store, was refurbished in 2017 using principles developed by AHMM to adapt industrial buildings for contemporary office use.

Establishing Principles

These principles recognise that those original early 20th-century buildings were built at a time when the use of commercial space was changing as fast as it is now. New technology then (mechanical) was having as big an impact on how companies worked as new technology now (digital). Large, open floor plates were needed to allow the flexibility necessary to adapt: this is the flexibility we need for our fast-changing businesses now. Ceiling heights were generous (at least 3.5 metres (11.5 feet)), opening windows provided cooling long before air-conditioning systems were available, and expressed concrete frames offered a passive cooling/warming system – all very attractive to us now in our environmentally conscious times.

Understanding how those principles, created a century ago and offered again by redesign and reuse, could be applied to new-build projects has resulted in the White Collar Factory building in London's Old Street for Derwent London (completed 2017). This building not only demonstrates what is possible by using principles developed for another purpose in another time, but that the resulting quality of accommodation, though delivering less overall floor space, provides greater financial value – triumphant evidence to support an argument little understood in many other sectors of commercial development.

The White Collar Factory on London's Old Street Roundabout – the culmination of a set of principles set out by Simon Allford years previously for the redevelopment of existing buildings. Here, applied to a virtual new-build.

AHMM,
White Collar Factory,
London,
2017

The building not only demonstrates what is possible by using principles developed for another purpose in another time, but that the resulting quality provides greater financial value

On a tight site, the development of office space and the leisure uses for its workers and surrounding residential communities define this complex, efficient scheme.

Of course, the successful execution of a set of carefully thought-through principles is one way. Another is to enjoy the serendipity of needs-must. At the Tea Building in Shoreditch, again for Derwent London (completed 2004), the delivery of a building that has been a model for industrial redevelopment since it was first converted is a perfect example. A canny buy for Derwent – a large, flexible building at the centre of an emerging district in Central East London – the Tea Building is in a location that was about to experience huge change. Not wanting to commit to a long-term strategy for the building until it was clear how the area would turn out, AHMM's scheme – developed from a brief to produce a speedy, low-cost solution for the temporary reuse of a former industrial building – has become a model copied the world over. The refurbishment of the industrial lifts (since replaced), the reverence for the bare internal concrete surfaces, the installation of low-cost industrial lighting solutions and the celebration of all the building's scars and foibles, set a tone for what is now a ubiquitous style of office building, indivisible from local strategies to turn former industrial areas of cities into zones of start-up innovation.

The late Anita Roddick of The Body Shop always talked of the innovation created by her company in the 1980s as simply a response to the fact that she had no money to develop her business – just very clever ingenuity and an ability to make so much out of nothing. The dark green of her stores that became so famous around the world was the only colour that would cover the damp on the walls of her first shop in Brighton. That you could buy any product in five or six bottle sizes was a result of the fact her bottle supplier ran out of the core size and she did not have enough bottles to fill her shelves. Her groundbreaking refill policy was simply a function of her inability to afford enough new bottles to satisfy demand as her fledgling business grew. These business innovations, that are now, still, the subject of Harvard Business School case studies, are no less clever for their development through necessity. The ingenuity that created them and recognised in them something that could define a business as it grew is the same ingenuity that delivered the Tea Building and its consequent impact on offices everywhere.

These early opportunities offered raw materials for the crucible of ideas which would eventually produce the portfolio of projects that define the globally significant practice AHMM has become.

AHMM's scheme
– developed from a
brief to produce
a speedy, low-cost
solution for the
temporary reuse of
a former industrial
building – has
become a model
copied the world over

Designed as a quick fix for a building that would be 'properly' redeveloped later, AHMM's scheme for the Tea Building became a sector-defining, game-changing refit. Early use of a shipping container, now much copied, defined the mood of the building on arrival.

The Tea Building in London's
Shoreditch – a strategically
important site in an area
undergoing massive
transformation. The building's
refit by AHMM led the creative
resurgence of the area.

AHMM,
Tea Building,
London,
2004

Trophy Headquarters Are Gone

What is important to recognise though, is that unlike so many other practices who have reached a similar scale over the same time, it is not that easy to recognise an AHMM building from a cursory glance. Their desire to create a body of work from a series of everyday buildings in cities that can, through clever design and a professional methodology, be made extraordinary is what sets them apart and defines their contribution to the modern office building idiom. Their interest in developing a response to the opportunity to reuse old buildings, add new buildings to complement them and create entirely new buildings based on an insatiable curiosity for how people want to work means their portfolio of completed projects is as diverse as it is large.

The days of the trophy headquarters building are long gone – progressive companies are far more interested in expressing their values through the quality of the environments they commission for their staff to work in. Far more attention is paid to the capacity for newly commissioned buildings to be adaptable over time, to conform to the highest environmental standards – both in performance and in embodied carbon – and to provide the opportunity for companies to enrich the physical and mental health of their employees. This requires an approach that is about as far from showy as possible and starts with an understanding of people and their daily lives, not the aesthetics of a particular architectural style. AHMM's approach to the design of their office buildings has always been rooted in the experience and needs of the people who will use them now and in the future.

Of course, no commercial office building will ever leave its CAD files unless it is capable of being built to a viable financial agenda set by its commissioning developer. An approach to designing commercial office buildings can consequently go one of two ways: start with a dream and deliver a finished building that is more often than not a disappointing shadow of its original ambition as cost-saving drives creative decision-making; or start with an approach that employs design innovation to engineer cost savings or end-value uplift. It is extraordinary how many buildings are the result of a battle between an architect, their client and a contractor rather than a collaboration to offer, through innovation, a perfect solution to a set of end users. At its best, this comes from long, successful relationships between architect and client, driven by a shared ambition to deliver quality buildings.

The days of the trophy headquarters building are long gone – progressive companies are far more interested in expressing their values through the quality of the environments they commission for their staff to work in

AHMM,
Television Centre,
London,
2018

How to create a new place in West London
retaining a sense of the heritage of one of the
UK's most famous buildings without designing
a nostalgic pastiche? Through understated
intervention that respected history rather than
celebrated it.

Now we have a greater chance to drive change than we have had in a very long time

Of course it is impossible to write anything about building commercial office space at the moment without returning to the subject that is on everyone's lips right now: how will our development projects need to change to accommodate the shift in working patterns inspired by our recovery from the coronavirus crisis? The immediate issue of how to cope with continued social distancing as we return to some form of normality is less important than how, in the longer term, we are going to be able to accommodate a vastly increased interest in more flexible home/office working patterns. We do not have the answers yet, but we know how we are going to find them – by listening, understanding what people want and responding creatively.

There is nothing new here that we need to do. What the coronavirus pandemic has offered us is simply the chance to address the issues that those, like AHMM, who have always been interested in innovating, have been advocating all along. Now we have a greater chance to drive change than we have had in a very long time. We should be taking the opportunity to ask our workforces what they want. How have they developed their thinking about the opportunity to significantly improve their quality of life by changing the way they work? But that is only half the story. The response has to come from the decades of thinking and innovation, locked up in design practices everywhere, that have the best opportunity in years to be set free. Those practices, like AHMM, whose working methods feed off adaptability to change and thrive on the opportunity to create flexibility for the future are the ones who will win. ⌂

AHMM,
Westminster Academy at
the Naim Dangoor Centre,
London,
2007

AHMM's interest in their idea of 'universality of use',
providing future flexibility of space and function,
has configured this secondary school academy as
a series of connected spaces that are both creative
opportunities as well as more traditional classrooms.

Ellis Woodman

opening up educating institutions,

AHMM has significant expertise in designing architecture for educational purposes. **Ellis Woodman** is an architecture critic and curator and the Director of the Architecture Foundation in London. He surveys this aspect of the practice, particularly in relation to the freeing up and creation of accessible, social space to learn within.

opening up methodologies

To chance on the aftermath of an internal review at AHMM's offices in Clerkenwell, London, is to encounter a studio culture defined by its commitment to decision-making through the exploration of multiple design iterations. Invariably projects are developed from the definition of strategic goals and the subsequent testing of option upon option against them. Such an open and discursive design methodology is perhaps a prerequisite for the smooth operation of a practice of AHMM's size: creative activity in an office of 500 people necessarily takes a different form from that which we might associate with an individual labouring privately in a sketchbook. But the strengths of such an open and fundamentally rational process are not solely measurable in terms of improved internal communications. AHMM determinedly frame the act of design as a sustained conversation, and this also represents a commitment to accommodate the contributions of others.

Patient Inclusivity

The appeal of this way of working is clear from the practice's many longstanding commercial clients: AHMM remains one of the most successful architects of housing and offices operating in the UK today. However, the work that best exemplifies the strengths of its patient and inclusive approach are the buildings it has delivered for institutions. The practice has been particularly active in the education sector and here it has often found itself navigating briefs freighted by the interests of multiple stakeholders and daunting programmatic complexity. In the case of two recent projects, the Stirling Prize-winning Burntwood School in South London (2014) and the long-gestating redevelopment of the University of Amsterdam's Roeterseiland campus (2018), the design challenges were further exacerbated by the fact that each represented a reworking of an architecturally distinguished but functionally problematic complex of postwar buildings. Both schemes testify to AHMM's capacity to achieve a consensus in the face of a vast range of seemingly competing concerns.

Burntwood School accommodates a community of 2,000 girls and 200 staff on a campus in suburban Wandsworth, which, prior to AHMM's interventions, comprised a series of standalone buildings of varied height and footprint dating from the 1950s. The largest were two four-storey blocks that accommodated most of the classrooms. Faced in precast concrete panels and expansive horizontal bands of glazing, these structures distributed teaching spaces down long double-loaded corridors. Their thermal and acoustic performance failed to satisfy contemporary standards, while the school had come to regard their cramped and repetitive plans as a significant constraint on its freedom to structure the curriculum. Compounded by the demand for an increase in school places, these considerations prompted the decision to embark on the buildings' comprehensive redevelopment.

AHMM's project would ultimately see the phased demolition not only of these, but also four other

AHMM, Burntwood School, Wandsworth, London, 2014

bottom: Burntwood revitalises, 'phoenix-like', a 1950s Modernist educational campus, creating accommodation for 2,000 pupils and 200 staff.

The school buildings are given a particular elevational treatment, configured by the 7.5-metre (24.6-foot) structural grid and the ability to exploit views, sunlight and shadow, to form an instantly recognisable façade regime.

Six new pavilions were constructed that augment the retained buildings and mature landscape, making a logical connection between them as well as articulating both the efficient use of space, but equally delight.

Burntwood School accommodates a community of 2,000 girls and 200 staff on a campus in suburban Wandsworth, which, prior to AHMM's interventions, comprised a series of standalone buildings of varied height and footprint dating from the 1950s

buildings on the site, sparing only the two most architecturally significant – a particularly elegant steel-framed assembly hall by Sir Leslie Martin and a concrete-framed swimming pool and gymnasium block. These retained structures are now integrated into a composition with six new blocks, variously housing classrooms, a dining room and sports facilities. Collectively they adopt a loose chequerboard arrangement, structured around a central covered pedestrian route that extends on a continuous axis from one end of the site to the other. Perhaps the project's principal attraction is the intimate relationship it cultivates between its constituent blocks and the adjacent outdoor spaces. It is an arrangement notably at odds with much recent school building in the UK, where the cost of land, the economy of construction and even school management considerations all tend to favour the consolidation of any academic brief into a single building. The architectural opportunities inherent in that premise are not wide. As Paul Monaghan once remarked, the plans of nearly all recent schools can be categorised as belonging to one of two types: the prison or the squashed cat.

The fact that an altogether richer spatial arrangement was achieved at Burntwood can largely be attributed to the requirement that the new buildings be constructed while the school remained in operation. This necessitated a six-phase programme of realisation in which the first new buildings had to be constructed on the school's open games court before the first of the older ones could be decanted and demolished. By accepting this logistical complexity, the school avoided incurring the costs of moving into temporary accommodation and directed those savings into the realised scheme.

The need to build in a manner that caused the least possible disruption to the school community was also a strong determinant in the choice of construction method. The commission followed a number of school projects in which AHMM had explored the use of loadbearing precast-concrete components, and the façades of the four classroom blocks at Burntwood push the expressive possibilities of this technology to new heights. Extending from floor to floor, the façade panels are alternately of 3-metre and 4.5-metre (9.8- and 14.8-foot) width, enabling them to be combined so as to correspond to the buildings' 7.5-metre (24.6-foot) structural module. Their monumental scale is further enforced by very pronounced modelling. Each incorporates a single large window set 400 millimetres (15.75 inches) back from the panel's leading edge, the concrete surface effectively forming a frame of splayed reveals. A comparison can be drawn with the façades of Marcel Breuer's 1970 buildings for the University of Massachusetts, but the surface treatment of the Burntwood blocks is more refined and the range of panel configurations far wider than the technology of half a century ago would have allowed.

The consistent treatment of the black-and-white façades provides a neutral backdrop for a landscape

AHMM,
Roeterseiland Campus,
University of Amsterdam,
2018

The project was fundamentally about opening up the city and campus both visually and physically, something the previous masterplan struggled with. This included cutting a larger void into the canal-spanning bridge building.

The main circulation routes of the campus were rearticulated from first-floor to ground level, bringing better and more varied possibilities of pedestrian access and closeness to landscape.

treatment of unusual richness. Building on the presence of a number of existing mature trees, the grounds have been developed in contrasting bands laid parallel to the central pedestrian spine. Spaces accessed directly off this route are articulated as a variety of squares, gardens and lawns, while land closer to the site's edge is given a more informal treatment. Through considerations of planting, surface finish, intimacy and adjacency the ground becomes a territory rich in opportunity for study, play and socialising. The image of the buildings and the life that goes on between them are inextricably linked.

Opening Up the Ground Plane
Built in the early 1960s, the University of Amsterdam's teaching facilities at Roeterseiland are broadly contemporaneous with Burntwood's original buildings, but represent a very different kind of campus. Located on the edge of Amsterdam's 19th-century Outer Ring, their site is defined by a denser urban context while the buildings themselves – which are used by as many as 20,000 students each day – are of a more imposing scale again. Conceived as a variety of megastructure, they were designed by Norbert Gawronski of Amsterdam's Public Works Department. Their dominant feature is a vast slab block that runs east–west across the site, traversing a north–south canal along the way. Gawronski designated the first floor as the principal pedestrian level and designed a series of adjacent towers on podiums that would plug into this network. However, in the years following the cultural upheavals of May 1968, the university's estate strategy shifted to one based on the refurbishment of buildings in the city's historic centre. Gawronski's project was left partially completed, rendering its already questionable relationship to the surrounding city still more dysfunctional.

By the turn of the century it had become clear that the image presented by the Roeterseiland buildings was damaging the university's efforts to compete in the lucrative international student market, while the technical performance of buildings that were now half a century old demanded urgent upgrading. In 2009, a competition was therefore launched to find an architect who could refurbish and remodel the campus. The programme of activities the university wanted to accommodate remained only sketchily defined, but AHMM's pitch ultimately succeeded thanks to its recognition that the buildings' fundamental problems lay in the inadequacy of their relationship to the wider city.

Gawronski's raised circulation had effectively killed off the street-life around the buildings, and one of AHMM's key ambitions was to reassert it through the articulation of a new ground-level thoroughfare extending along the canal. The significance of this route – which enjoys a similar status to the covered pedestrian route at Burntwood – is emphasised by a series of related interventions, the most dramatic of which is the excavation of a five-storey void from the slab block at the point that it bridges the water. In opening up an expansive view of the surrounding city, this gesture emphasises the buildings' metropolitan scale, but also draws the lower buildings that line the canal into a much more considered compositional relationship – the fact that the height of the cut corresponds to their eaves level is particularly significant in this regard.

AHMM has provided new façades for each of Gawronski's buildings, subtly distinguishing them through their varied horizontal and vertical emphasis and modulation within a close palette of blacks and greys. As in the original design, their expression remains fundamentally serial but leavened by AHMM's habitual impulse towards pattern-making. Approaching the slab block we discover the black aluminium cladding panels are of contrasting matt and gloss finish, while the internal concrete structure visible through the full-height windows has been painted in a range of citrus colours in recognition of the presence of different departmental 'houses'.

Counterintuitively, these façades appear at their lightest and most transparent at the very point where the building has to accommodate the most structure – the moment of bridging the canal. It is here that we find the largest and most representational volume in the whole complex – a social space, dubbed the 'City Room', sized to accommodate up to 200 people. The massive steel box girder required to span the canal runs down its centre, liberating the space from columns and enabling a fully glazed double-height façade of great delicacy to be suspended from above. Particularly at night the space functions as a powerful signal of the university's civic function.

But it is the reclamation of the ground plane as a place of public congregation that arguably ranks as the scheme's most transformative achievement.

The practice has been very explicit about its ambitions to court an ambiguity between school and office

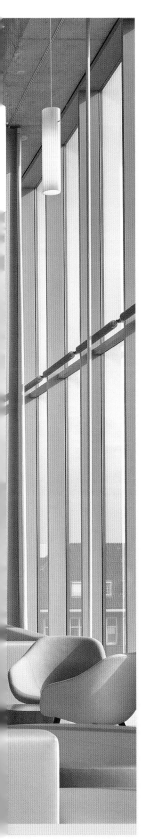

AHMM,
Westminster Academy at
the Naim Dangoor Centre,
London,
2007

The academy is a colourful presence in
its immediate area, highly visible due
to its glass panels and coloured bands
of terracotta tiles.

AHMM,
Roeterseiland Campus,
University of Amsterdam,
2018

Internal spaces are light and airy, the whole
campus animated by colour to produce
convivial spaces for meeting and learning,
fully equipped for modern education.

The change is signalled by gestures such as the introduction of extensive glazing into the buildings' formerly solid plinth, and a broad and low-slung pedestrian bridge at the point where the slab has been extracted. A generous new entrance pavilion serving the whole complex is sited alongside, for the first time locating the front door at the level of the street. The scene that these few strategic moves conjure into being is a distinctly theatrical one. Its foreground is populated by students chatting by the banks of the canal or making their way to classes across the new bridge, while the city beyond is revealed like a backcloth glimpsed through a proscenium.

A Matter of Architectural Language
As at Burntwood, the architectural language that AHMM deploys at Roeterseiland suggests a strong connection with postwar American Modernism of a kind that moved easily between corporate and academic cultures. Indeed, in describing past projects such as the Westminster Academy at the Naim Dangoor Centre in London (2007), the practice has been very explicit about its ambitions to court an ambiguity between school and office, and similar claims might be made for the two schemes considered here. Resisting the adoption of familiar signals of functional or contextual identity, AHMM's interventions remain unimpeachably abstract, optimistic and modern, succeeding in communicating their role as civic institutions thanks to their emphatic adoption of human occupation in the foreground of each project's image. Their programme will doubtless fluctuate over time, but AHMM has inscribed a deep structure into each of these sites that will ensure their legibility as places of public congregation remains. ◬

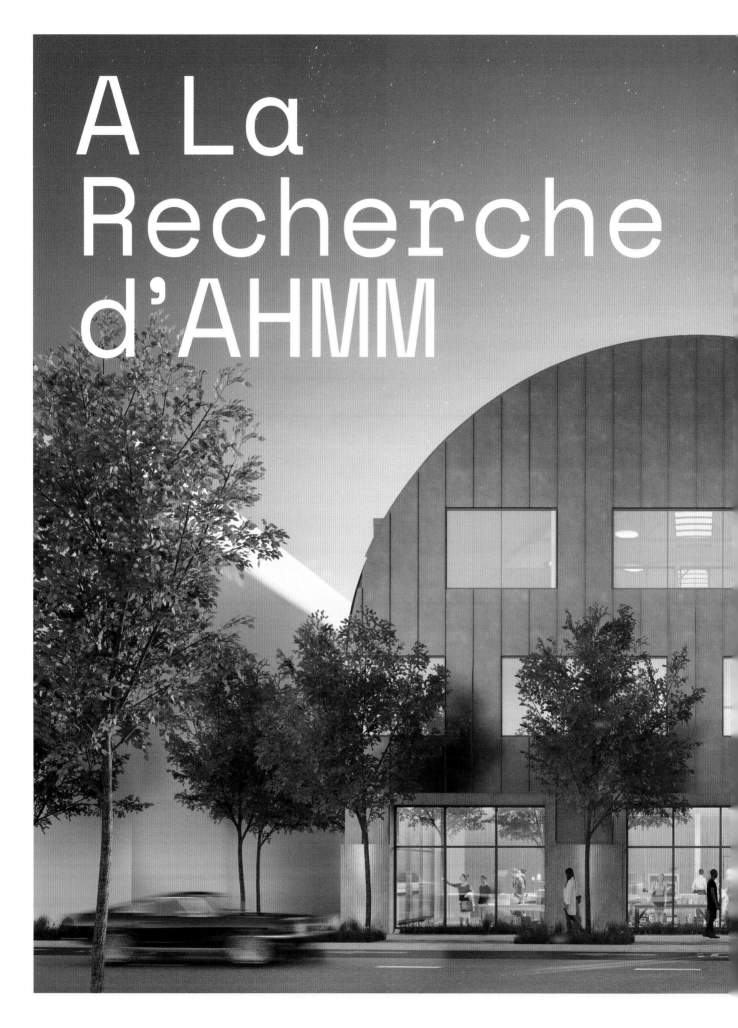

A La Recherche d'AHMM

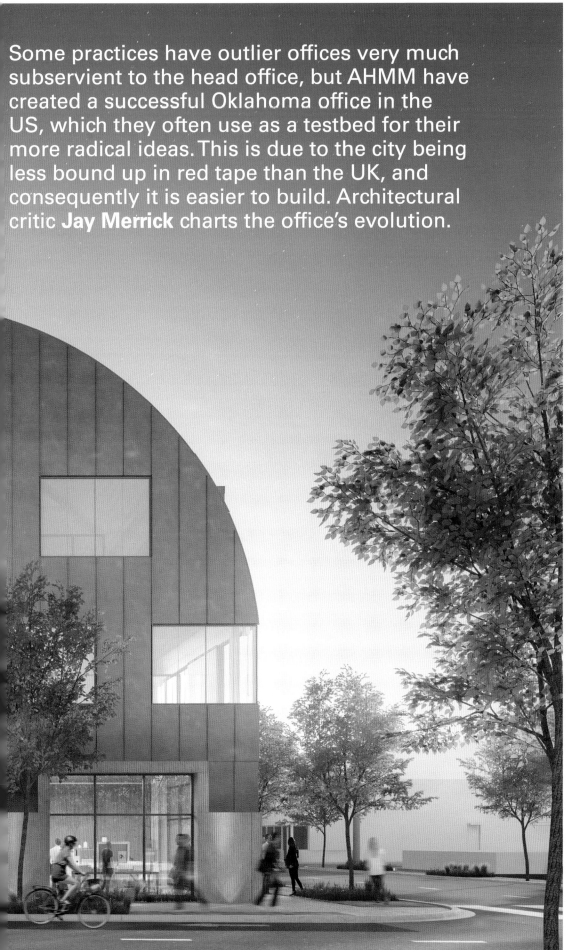

Jay Merrick

Some practices have outlier offices very much subservient to the head office, but AHMM have created a successful Oklahoma office in the US, which they often use as a testbed for their more radical ideas. This is due to the city being less bound up in red tape than the UK, and consequently it is easier to build. Architectural critic **Jay Merrick** charts the office's evolution.

AHMM,
Block 13,
Wheeler District,
Oklahoma City,
design in progress,
2021–2

This three-storey mixed-use office and retail building is on a private airfield site dating back to 1947, and so the design takes the form of an elegantly detailed, barrel-vaulted 'hangar' that sits on a masonry-faced ground-floor podium.

In 2019 I suggested in *D* that Allford Hall Monaghan Morris's projects in Oklahoma City had 'an interesting *à la recherche de l'aventure perdue* quality' that had modulated the practice's commercial image.[1] It seemed to me that some practices that become very successful – AHMM is currently Britain's third biggest, generating annual fees of more than £50m – must yearn to re-experience something of the risks and primal developments of their original architectural ideas.

I offer a handful of AHMM's early projects as scene-setters to begin to flesh out this suggestion, and the first must be Great Notley Primary School (1999) in Essex, the design of which still seems relatively radical. The building was environmentally and programmatically novel: triangular plan, substantial internal courtyard, turfed roof, saw-toothed rooflights, and a black 'Plimsoll line' of windows in the timber-clad walls.

AHMM won this project in a Design Council-led competition. 'We presented an attitude to the design,' explains Simon Allford. 'And when we started to design it, Essex County Council gave us their two-inch-thick design guide and said: "Give us a school that's better than this design guide." Our strategy was that if we were clever about the way the school could be used, it could also become a community building.[2]

'We wanted to make a building with bigger rooms and less circulation – a generosity of spaces, and a building with an optimistic Modernist profile. It's still one of the hardest working buildings we've ever designed and I hope there's something of Alberti's saying about it – that nothing can be added or taken away.'[3]

AHMM then delivered the Dalston Lane mixed-use building (1999) in northeast London for the charitable Peabody Trust. The design was constrained by an existing permission for a scheme that had been devised by cost consultants; which meant that factors such as height and the building envelope were set.

The strategic design question here was: How do you celebrate an ordinary building type, architecturally? The three upper apartment storeys were moved back 5 metres (16 feet), leaving the ground-floor shopfronts projecting forward to align with a neighbouring building line. More obviously striking were the chequerboards of big blue-and-white painted squares on the façades, a nod to the elevation graphics of council flats in Pimlico, London, designed by Sir Edwin Lutyens in 1929.

The Tea Building as a Loose-Fit Trigger
Five years later, in 2004, AHMM completed the first of a 21-year-long series of adaptations of the city-block-sized Tea Building in East London, which was originally a 19th-century warehouse. The scheme immediately became an influential archetype for the deliberately loose-fit internal volumes and fit-outs now typical for buildings designed or remodelled to house creative or business startups. The original Tea Building project was 'the first proper working building we designed', recalls Allford. 'We lied [to the developers] about how big we were. We were just the four partners and a few architectural students.'

AHMM,
Great Notley
Primary School,
Essex,
England,
1999

AHMM's inaugural project produced a radical building form generated by a strategy-led approach to design that has since become their modus operandi. The guiding idea was to make a building that could serve both educational and community uses, and this produced the unusual triangular plan, central court-yard and only one corridor.

AHMM,
Tea Building,
London,
2004

opposite: The building introduced so-called loose-fit, easily reconfigured workspaces within large ex-warehouses in Shoreditch, East London. The low-cost interventions and basic detailing that suited the then low-rent area have since become a default design approach to fashionable and profitable transformations of Victorian and Edwardian industrial hulks all over the UK.

The Tea Building block was composed of three warehouses, and initially the developers considered replacing one of them with a new building. But the project evolved into an exercise in very basic, minimum-cost treatments of volumes, structure, surfaces and environmental controls. As the phases proceeded, the building's internal structure was exposed, double-glazed windows were installed, the inner faces of the façades were insulated, and new lift shafts were inserted into lightwells. 'If a building has essentially good qualities,' says Allford, 'you can create these [new] working machines.'

The Tea Building was the conceptual trigger for AHMM's later, more architecturally sophisticated adaptations of big existing structures – most notably, in London, the Angel Building (2010) in Islington, and the White Collar Factory (2017) in Old Street. The design of the latter was developed using a jacked-up 3,000-square-foot (278-square-metre) prototype of the building costing well over £1 million, to prove that the low-tech environmental strategy would work. 'It was high-risk stuff', Allford admits, but ultimately the building proved to be worth substantially more than the developer's original projected commercial value.

Going Stateside
All of these projects were genuine adventures in design, developed in the uniquely British quicksands formed by the competing perceptions of planners, designers, developers, consultants and local authority committees. AHMM's early work survived these forces because of its strategy-first approach and what Allford describes as 'a strong affinity to making'. There was also, perhaps, the spirit of a remark made by Allford's architect father, David, in a speech at the Architectural Association (AA) in London in 1984: 'Without rational analysis at the root of your approach to design the work will be wilful, confused and meaningless.'[4]

In 2009, architectural work in the UK had collapsed, but the reverse was the case in Oklahoma City. In 1993, the city's first Metropolitan Area Projects to rebuild parts of the downtown area were under way; two years later, following the terror-bomb devastation of the Alfred P Murrah Federal Building, national and local regeneration funds began to flow into the city.

Before that, the city had suffered severe socio-economic fractures caused by the failure of IM Pei's 1965 Central Business District redevelopment plan. Many downtown retailers relocated in malls further out, leaving the city centre littered with empty buildings and lots – an ironic reminder of the boomtown days of the 1930s when one of the city's many housing advertisements announced: 'Crown Heights. This is your opportunity to CASH IN on Oklahoma City LOTS as low as $750.'

Simon Allford had first visited Oklahoma City in 2008, at the suggestion of one of AHMM's associate directors, Wade Scaramucci, an Oklahoman. And when Allford decided to try to develop projects in the city he was, in a sense, walking into the first page of the now legendary polemical essay in *New Society* magazine in 1969. The main heading read 'Non-Plan: An Experiment in Freedom', and the opening statement made a radical proposal: 'Town and country planning has today become an unquestioned shibboleth. Yet few of its procedures or value judgments have any sound basis, except delay. Why not have the courage, where practical, to let people shape their own environment?'[5]

A Novelty: Inventing Constraints
And something like this freedom – certainly compared to London – was the design and construction situation that AHMM encountered in Oklahoma City: 'A different world with different metrics, and virtually no consultants involved,' as Allford puts it. 'Here, we had to invent our own constraints. In London, you have to be ingenious to get around the constraints.'

Wade Scaramucci sets out the principles of their approach: 'We would only take on projects that were architecturally ambitious and had a real chance to change and impact the city. We would only take on a project if it was comprehensively done; in other words, we insisted on doing the outside and the inside [of buildings]. We would use Oklahoma City as a testbed of ideas – research that we could adapt and move between London and OKC.'[6]

In America's 25th biggest city, there is no Byzantine planning procedure: the client and architect propose a scheme, and if it meets the technical requirements for construction, functionality, and health and safety it can be approved. In more sensitive contexts, such as the historically significant Bricktown and Deep Deuce districts, the only additional hurdle is that designs must be presented to, and approved by, local oversight boards; the general public has very little influence on planning decisions. 'The architecture here is a little more near the edge,' explains Scaramucci. 'We're pushing things harder because we can. It's a city where, originally, there wasn't much thought about what buildings could give to the city. It was a city to be driven past at speed. It used to be the kind of place that was easy to leave because the economy was stagnant and the downtown was dead.'

Allford found that he 'had to learn a huge amount about the relationships of the grid to the city and to cars. Almost every plot is an isolated, acontextual island because of the cars.' One of AHMM's apartment block schemes in Oklahoma City counters the prevailing building block / parking lot urban chequerboard effect by positioning a multistorey car park as the central divider of the development's two internal courtyards.

AHMM have completed 22 buildings in Oklahoma City in the last 20 years, and 15 more are at various design or delivery stages. The types and scales of the finished projects – large-scale adaptive reuse, newbuild mixed-use, bars and eateries, architecturally svelte homes – seem precisely the kind that a young, thrusting practice would idealise as launchpads to more ambitious, high-profile commissions.

'We've tried to export our London-centric approach, developing stories about why we want to do what we do,' says Allford. 'They [clients and local oversight boards] enjoyed that. We have a belief in the pleasures of the urban street, which they're beginning to share – and the younger people here are more interested in urbanity.

'It's a much more innocent world, though some of our clients are seriously cosmopolitan and well-travelled. They all want to bring something to the city and leave it better than they found it.' AHMM's clients have ranged from a well-known hairdresser to some of the state's wealthiest and most significant individuals, industrialists and businesspeople; most had little or no previous professional experience of building projects.

Low-Tech and a Rough Vernacular
AHMM's first completed project in Oklahoma City, in 2011, was the $350,000 redevelopment of a very plain ex-Bible bindery into a two-family home (with a neon sign announcing 'Jesus Saves' on the main façade). A simple shift produced a new secondary façade set back from the original street-facing one, which shades the ground-floor glazing and creates a semi-screened balcony at the upper level. A sawtooth rooflight casts natural light into the mostly open-plan first floor, which has a balcony behind the window blanks of the original rear façade.

AHMM,
Jesus Saves,
Oklahoma City,
Oklahoma,
2011

The creation of a two-family dwelling in what had been a two-
storey bible bindery required interventions including a new
internal steel frame to preserve the original brick structure and
allow new internal volumes to be created without in any way
traducing the character of the original building.

AHMM's first completed
project in Oklahoma City,
in 2011, was the $350,000
redevelopment of a very
plain ex-Bible bindery into
a two-family home

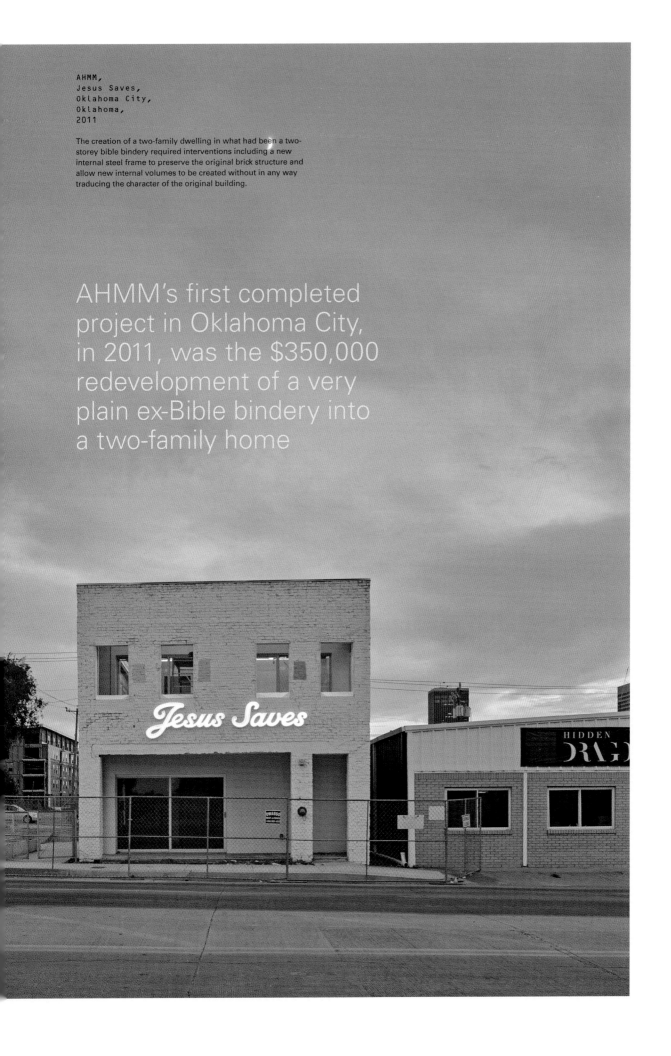

AHMM,
Squirrel Park,
Oklahoma City,
Oklahoma,
2018

Eight double-stacked shipping
containers, shifted slightly in plan,
produced four homes with a well-
shaded front porch and an upstairs
balcony. The careful treatment of
details, glazing and landscaping
has turned these simple functional
objects into attractive dwellings.

The plan and section are simple and carried out without
any elaborate detailing; the internal brickwork and the
original structure remain honestly exposed.

At an equally small scale, two schemes using
shipping containers were absolute novelties in the city,
though Allford sees a conceptual connection with a
quasi-Plug-In City in Oklahoma City – John Johansen's
remarkable, but now demolished Archigram-inspired
Mummers Theater (1970). The OKSea mixed-use
scheme (2014) features stacked containers, angled
against the urban grain of the site and adapted to
create work units and eateries on a once empty lot.
At Squirrel Park (2018), an engaging composition of
double-stacked containers, slightly shifted in plan,
has created an admirable tableau of homes in an
exemplary landscaping and planting scheme – the latter
a distinctive contributing feature of all AHMM's projects
in the city, which has prompted the practice to employ
a horticultural adviser for their British work.

In other Oklahoma City projects, design development
has absorbed and re-expressed local construction
vernaculars – most dramatically at the six mixed-
use blocks of the Classen 16 development (2018), the
elevations of which shimmer with scale-like aluminium
shakes. 'In construction,' says Allford, 'this is a land of
speed. There's a basic roughness.'

But pragmatic material ingredients can produce
elegant architecture – most notably at the AEP Fitness
Center / OKC Ballet (2015), where relatively delicate
arched-steel trusses hold up a gently radiused barrel
vault made with standard pleated industrial metal
sheeting. The internal composition of the racquetball
'box' and the open sports and ballet volumes
accentuates the crisply stripped-down minimalism of
the architecture.

AHMM,
AEP Fitness Center / OKC Ballet,
Oklahoma City,
Oklahoma,
2015

The site already had a raw basement box and steel arches, and was originally intended to become a secure repository for 250,000 bottles of vintage wine for one of the city's most famous industrialists. But he decided to develop the building as a sports centre for AEP employees, and when the firm closed, AHMM again repurposed it, this time into a ballet facility. The crude, heavy arches were replaced with lighter trussed arches supporting a folded steel skin, with fully glazed gable ends and well-composed interior elements.

The internal composition
of the racquetball 'box' and
the open sports and
ballet volumes accentuates
the crisply stripped-down
minimalism of the architecture

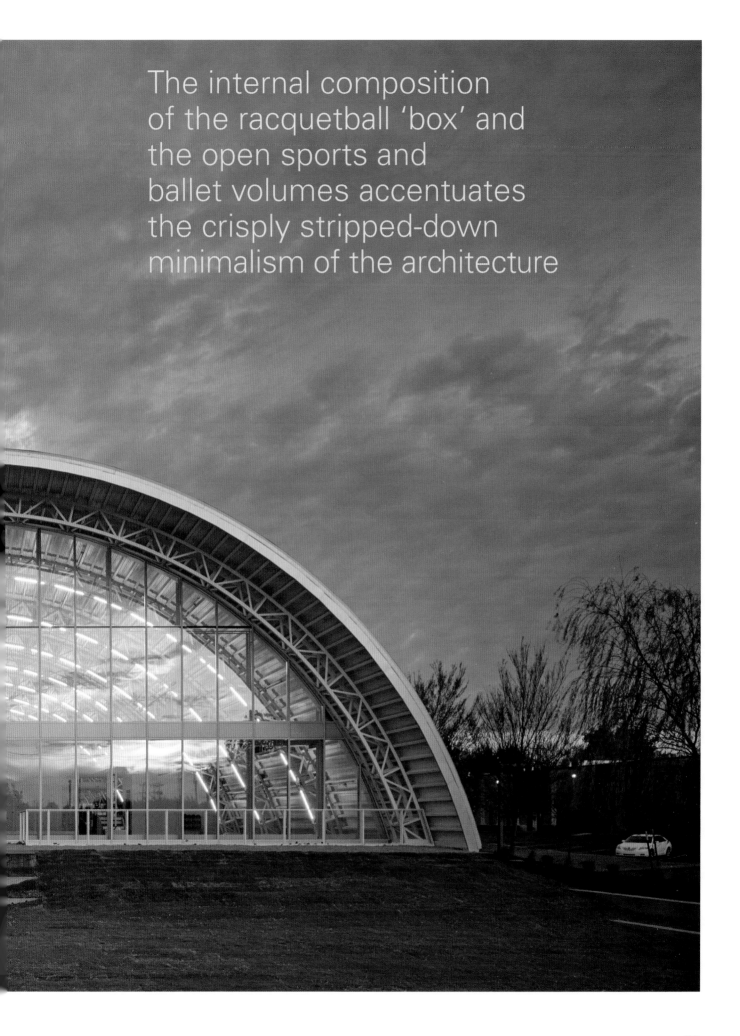

AHMM,
Bob Moore Auto Group headquarters,
Oklahoma City,
Oklahoma,
2015

The 1951 single-storey brick-clad structure had previously been extended and remodelled. The latest interventions pared the building back, and opened up and extended it upwards to create a modern working environment. Notable is the way light and landscaping reaches into parts of the site and the building.

AHMM,
The Bower OKC,
Oklahoma City,
Oklahoma,
2019

The design of the Bower brings a touch of New London Vernacular architecture to Oklahoma City, and two characteristics in particular: projecting patterns of brick, and interestingly articulated massing, with townhouses along the street line and multistorey condominium segments behind them.

Allford regards all of AHMM's buildings in the city as experiments. It will be interesting to see how this approach is affected by their increasing Oklahoman workload

In locally innovative adaptive reuse schemes such as the Bob Moore Auto Group office (2015), Eighth Street Market (2017) and Central Exchange (2019), AHMM's ability to combine cross-flowing interiors with engaging threshold sequences is very apparent. And in the forthcoming office and retail Block 13 in the city's developing Wheeler District (2021–2), the architecture is quite unexpected: a highly finessed three-storey variant of the humble Nissen hut that recalls the historic hangars on what had been a private airfield site.

In other projects, the treatments of forms and elevations are in something like the New London Vernacular manner – such as the tidy patterns of projecting brickwork in the luxurious Cumberland Court home (2019) and at the Bower OKC housing development (2019). In the latter, the massing skilfully combines a line of streetfront townhouses with higher, irregularly shouldered condominiums behind. The Grand Boulevard office building (2021) is equally London-centric: the elevation grid and double-height layers of the deliberately 'heavy' limestone frame are very strongly expressed, with deep-set glazing and cantilevered corners.

Allford regards all of AHMM's buildings in the city as experiments. It will be interesting to see how this approach is affected by their increasing Oklahoman workload. The practice's studio in the city, led by Scaramucci and overseen by Allford, is now developing much higher-profile cultural, educational, housing and masterplan projects. Ultimately, adds Allford, 'we want to produce architecture that's deeply rooted here'. It is a serendipitous remark. When Cedric Price, co-author of the 'Non-Plan' essay, saw Great Notley Primary School 21 years ago, he told Allford: 'The black Plimsoll line anchors the building to the landscape.' It is evidently hard to escape the gravities of early architectural adventurism. ⌂

Notes
1. Jay Merrick, 'The Image of Architects', in Laura Iloniemi, ⌂ The Identity of the Architect: Culture and Communication, Nov/Dec (no 6), 2019, p 114.
2. All quotes from Simon Allford are from noted conversations with Jay Merrick in June 2020.
3. Simon Allford paraphrases Leon Battista Alberti's remark about beauty as 'that reasoned harmony of all the parts within a body, so that nothing may be added, taken away or altered, but for the worse', which appears in On the Art of Building in Ten Books [1556], trans Joseph Rykwert with Neil Leach and Robert Tavernor, MIT Press (Cambridge, MA), 1992, p 156.
4. David Allford, 'À la Recherche du Temps Corbu', AA Files 6, Architectural Association (London), 1984, p 72.
5. Reyner Banham, Paul Barker, Peter Hall and Cedric Price, 'Non-Plan: An Experiment in Freedom', New Society, 20 March 1969, p 435. See also Sam Wetherell, 'Freedom Planned: Enterprise Zones and Urban Non-Planning in Post-War Britain', Twentieth Century British History, 27 (2), 2016, pp 266–89.
6. Wade Scaramucci, Complete and Future Projects in Oklahoma, FifthMan/AHMM (London), 2020, p 7. All other quotes from Wade Scaramucci are from noted conversations with Jay Merrick during June 2020.

AHMM,
100 Union Street,
London,
2018

above: The finished office
building, showing the propped
cantilever providing public space
as an extension of Union Street
towards the railway arches beyond.
Entering the building through
this space with blue-glazed bricks
and coloured props contrasting
with the plain façade provides an
enchanting approach.

Roger Zogolovitch,
concept sketch for
100 Union Street,
Southwark,
London,
2017

A concept sketch made during
a breakfast meeting with Simon
Allford of AHMM – sketching
as a means of collaborative
communication.

Roger Zogolovitch

The Invention of Projects that Create an Address

Roger Zogolovitch, founder and Creative Director of Solidspace, and AHMM founding director Simon Allford have had a decades-long relationship developing ideas and building together. Over the years their friendship has been consolidated by fine dining and a mutual respect that has made Solidspace a serial client. And one where architect and client work as a symbiotic whole. Here Zogolovitch writes of their kipper breakfast meetings and of two recent developments for apartments and offices in South-East London.

My relationship with Simon Allford has developed, partly, over breakfast meetings. Imagine familiar London restaurants in the background with grilled kippers in the foreground. The challenge of extracting the flesh from the bone instantly raises aroma and lifts the expectation around the table. It is a setting where 'new thinking' can flourish.

This routine has existed for decades. Respective personal assistants have been flummoxed with meeting places that were referred to as 'our corner' or 'that café slightly west of Marylebone High Street that served a perfect kipper' for our meetings. In total over a hundred breakfasts have been had.

They are relevant to the story as they cement the success of the client/architect relationship. They established the means of communication for a collaborative approach. It is to the benefit of Simon's client rapport that he was prepared to facilitate this way of working together.

Meetings were also conducted in more conventional settings – office based, with all consultants, agendas and development managers taking minutes. While this is the standard format it undermines the idea of collaboration. Such meetings inevitably become combative and force client and consultant to take sides. One side retains the mask of commerciality, the other preserves their professional and design defence. This invariably results in known outcomes and low-risk management practice and continues the status quo.

Architect and Client – A Collaboration
The ambition has been to forge a new mutual relationship between architect and developer, to drive a creative process and extend such promise to all aspects of our projects. The dynamic of this relationship is more like that between a restaurateur and a chef. Simon and his team at AHMM supported these endeavours to manage the projects collectively.

Simon and I share memories of Cedric Price who taught us both the critical importance of the 'idea' at the core of a worthy project. The strength of that idea became the driver. The desire to generate convivial and efficient but delightful apartments and offices was the guiding idea behind Weston Street (2018) and 100 Union Street (2018), to create recognisable addresses for people to live and work in. A direct form of communication with new rules needed to be developed to deliver them. The closer and easier the personal relationship became, the more the reliance on each other to keep faith with that original idea – checking with each other and accepting that we were both originators and critics.

In the world of commercial development, many constraints and risks demand resolution to allow the project to proceed. Advice floods in from different disciplines, from business to design, each jostling for pole position. Keeping the idea intact from inception through to completion remains a challenge.

Working with a client who is both an architect and developer is a challenge. Making projects as a continuation of research is a provocation. The benefit of our working relationship shared the commitment to these principles and made them enjoyable.

Reading and Responding to the Context
The two projects inhabit Southwark, in London, SE1. The origins of this area date back to the medieval city whose two halves were linked by a single crossing over the Thames. Both sites – Weston Street and Union Street – are located 500 metres (550 yards) from London Bridge. Walking through the area today people can still sense those remnants in a street pattern overlaid with 19th-century infrastructure. This gives the area its historical ambience. The Crossbones site on Union Street, for example, is the remains of a medieval graveyard for the city's poor and outcast; and the wall marking the boundary of the infamous Marshalsea debtors' prison also still contributes to the urban atmosphere. This was the setting for us to make our contribution to the fabric of the city.

On Union Street, an archaeological investigation was conducted and at 3 metres (10 feet) below the current street level the contents of Roman 'bin bags' were found – oyster shells. At Weston Street, while excavating down for a lift shaft below the 3-metre datum for the water table, the site flooded with tidal water from the Thames.

Victorian infrastructure brought elevated railways 8 metres (26 feet) above ground on viaducts supported by arches, leaving sites on their edges. Our Union Street site was just that, a long strip of land lying between the street and the railway.

The Weston Street site was enclosed to the south with a fragment of an 18th-century brick wall. This historic boundary wall was retained and the building designed to appear to emerge above it. The beautifully patinated old bricks were left as a relic, a recognition of the memory of the history embedded in our new building.

This description of the sites as the setting for our projects represents the backdrop of the tough urbanism that drove our architectural response. Here is part of the original brief that describes the initial intention:

> My position is somehow to keep at the front of our minds some perspective. This site (Weston St) is rare and a gem. It is an extraordinary canvas on which we can all work to make a wonderful piece of city. We own it and control it, in a perfect world we should be able to carve and create a development on it entirely as our imaginations dictate. We won't be able to do that because of the constraints of P&R [planning and regulation]. However we must start from the position of inspiration and develop our own ideas that make the site worthy of the effort that we will all have to give to make this development a reality. Let's make sure that we stand above the complex P&R position and declare ourselves for the site. We are making something together which is our contribution to demonstrate a balanced and inspired development, which can in a genuine way be a home for the occupiers to live and work.

The retained fragment of 18th-century wall embedded in the construction, with the new apartments building emerging above it – a visual reminder of this historic location in Southwark's Bermondsey neighbourhood.

AHMM,
81-87 Weston Street,
Southwark,
London,
2018

Expressive cantilevered deep balconies leading from volumetric spaces become rooms which extend the experience of 'calm and comfortable space' connected with the interior. The exterior also provides a contemporary addition to the surrounding conservation context.

AHMM,
81-87 Weston Street,
Southwark,
London,
2018

The interior space, with the three
levels of the Solidspace DNA
'eat live work' expressed in a
palette of board-marked in-situ
concrete walls and bespoke oak-
veneer furniture, represents the
elegance and resolution of the
'slow-build' approach.

Zogolovitch (left) and Allford (right) managed throughout to check with each other to make certain that the project remained faithful to the original intention and avoided compromise.

Patience to Achieve Slow Building

Simon appreciated the role of the client as decision-maker and his acceptance of the spirit of this endeavour became a personal prop in delivering the project. His tolerance for my passion for concrete, hands-on control and forensic examination to every corner of the building and his determined and persistent support allowed the projects to become reality. Decision-making was driven by confidence that the vision, for these two projects, made collaboratively was coherent and had its own integrity. This resulted in innovative strong ideas for new architecture in the city.

They both represent cutting-edge, passive low-carbon technology using thermal mass to create stable, comfortable living and working conditions. The design provides atmosphere in its material palette and luminescence in its use of opening windows, and creates a generosity of space using volume, all contributing to provide calm and comfortable interior spaces for the occupants to live and work in. In these projects we both made an entirely new and contemporary addition as our positive and respectful contribution to the city.

The buildings represent a long and successful collaborative relationship with AHMM, Simon and his team. These were slow-build projects, much like slow cooking – elaborate and painstaking in the making, wonderful in the savouring. The analogy to food, restaurants and chefs luckily breaks down as we manage to leave behind the triumph of our joint enterprise and watch as the schemes mature to become 'development as art'. ⏎

In these projects we both made an entirely new and contemporary addition as our positive and respectful contribution to the city

BEING SIGNI

THE PROBLEM OF WHAT WE CAN

Hanif Kara

FICANT

NOT MEASURE

```
AHMM,
240 Blackfriars Road,
Southwark, London,
2014
```

The 90-metre (295-foot) tall,
20-storey office tower is topped
with a triple-height 'sky room'
and forms a crystalline object
playing off its sister, a smaller,
dark masonry residential
block, on London's skyline.
Both buildings are cut away to
afford generous public realms
at their bases.

Hanif Kara is co-founder of London-based international structural engineering firm AKT II. He is also Professor in Practice of Architectural Technology at Harvard University Graduate School of Design. He describes his ongoing working relationship with AHMM, stretching back over two decades, the qualities of which include mutual respect, friendship and a little healthy competition.

AHMM,
CASPAR Housing,
Birmingham, England,
1999

The two multistorey blocks of single-occupancy flats are connected by a glazed seam of lightweight bridges. These provide individual access to each of the 46 one- and two-bedroom flats, and were invented to afford privacy by replacing shared decks. Natural light is maximised by their staggered positions at the scheme's centre. The project was conceived to posit a protype for urban living.

Architects require a broad knowledge base in order to master their craft, and the discipline has a long history of alliances with many intellectual domains: the arts and sciences, ethics, social sciences and political philosophy. In recent history, architects have also embraced methodologies from fields such as sociology, anthropology, linguistics, literary criticism and structuralism.

Structural integrity, however, is a basic requirement of any functional built structure and architecture that does not address structure is incomplete and illogical. This philosophy has been at the core of AKT II's conversations with Simon Allford and AHMM over the last 20 years, allowing us to produce good buildings together, in a culture of collaborative autonomy that strengthens each of our practices.

As an engineer I am interested in luminaries such as Ove Arup, Felix Samuely and Ted Happold who practised in the second half of the 20th century. As did they, I feel that creating buildings is more about the synthesis of many disciplines and less about 'heroic engineering'. This contradicted the prevailing late 20th- to early 21st-century fashion of labelling buildings as 'sculptural', 'iconic' and 'functional', and typecasting architects as 'delivery architects', 'architectural designers', and 'artistic consultants', obscuring what architecture is and can be.

The Power of the Digital

Both AHMM and AKT II flourished during this time, which was also when new technologies began to expand the toolkit of architects and engineers. In the early 1990s, designers began to wholeheartedly embrace the new-found power of digital technology and the freedom it offered. We were among the engineers who were its early adopters, utilising tools and technologies that used self-governing parameters to create formal designs with our convincing and pervasive analytics.

It was against this background that our relationship with AHMM was forged, both of us searching for relief from cliché and a retreat towards shared interests, the most important being that we both wanted to get things built. Our exchanges clarified the pernicious effect of the battle between the architectural and engineering professions, those who construct what we draw, and the clients who pay us all.

Our first collaborative project brought these interests into sharp focus. CASPAR (City-Centre Apartments for Single People at Affordable Rents) Housing in Birmingham (1999) is a low-cost exemplar; a competition-winning 'develop and construct' affordable housing scheme with an absolutely precise integration of function, form and budget. In hindsight, it set up a shorthand, no-nonsense, back-to-basics approach to generating ideas, armed with a presupposition of familiarity with construction that would stand up to the industry's 'nice, but cannot be built' mantra.

It is relevant that as an engineering design office, this was approximately the same time that we won our first project with Will Alsop: The Public, a multipurpose arts building in Sandwell, West Midlands, that took many years to build (completed 2008) and with Zaha Hadid: the Hoenheim-Nord Terminus and Car Park in Strasbourg, France (2001). I was jolted out of complacency by these three collaborations, realising that as design engineers our alliances must go beyond the technical aspects of 'solving problems' to absorbing and endorsing multiple positions in architecture, including such unquantifiable qualities as 'beauty'. What we learned from our exposure to these architects' very different design approaches, contributed to the success of the alignment we enjoy with AHMM today.

AHMM were full of curiosity, generous, gently competitive and discreet; they would probably deny any interest in who else we were working with. At Adelaide Wharf, our next project, in Hackney, London (2007), another developer-led low-cost housing building, we were able to further some of AHMM's ideas for CASPAR using prefabrication systems to complete an elegant award-winning scheme.

The Fruits of Early Thinking

It was during the design of the Yellow Building offices (Kensington and Chelsea, 2008), offices and residential 240 Blackfriars Road (Southwark, 2014) and the Angel Building (Islington, 2010), all in London, that we began to see the fruits of our early thinking. AHMM took a leap in 'creative intelligence and professionalism', having understood the needs of the new knowledge worker and the kind of vision that required both analytical thinking and architectural imagination. Conversations with Simon about 'the idea' became dominant, intense and more frequent. The roles of transmitter and receiver of practical and intellectual knowledge alternated often during one-to-one design sessions through to conceptualisation. London was booming, but still lacked clients that were interested in design. Utility as a concept became a resource for design ideas.

AHMM succeeded in packaging their approach as a demonstration of intellectual curiosity and an understanding of contemporary culture, to invent new workspaces in areas of London needing 'a new effect'. They were able to seize this opportunity, at the right time and in the right place, having acquired their unique design approach by actively concentrating in this field with an appreciation of open problems of design, in particular pertaining to workspaces of the future. They could put clients at the centre of the project without 'selling out' their own ideas about architecture, uniting innovative concepts with knowledge of what can be built, to get a return on investment with incremental innovations in each project.

Our first conversations would typically start over breakfast or a quick design session: fast, furious and fearless sketches by Simon to test his ideas (rarely was it a blank sheet – it was always clear that he had already thought of the big ideas) with my reactions as 'his engineer' jumping off from the response to our brief. The design obstacles and exchanges would generate more ideas. The next meeting would be a week or so

AHMM,
Yellow Building,
Kensington and Chelsea,
London,
2008

The new office building is structurally light, its internal and external architecture defined by a diagonal concrete grid developed in collaboration with AKT II that wraps around it to provide structural rigidity. Refined and economical, the structure requires no supporting cores.

AHMM,
Angel Building, Islington,
London, 2010

An example of AHMM's ability to rejuvenate
fragmented, forgotten older buildings by
transforming them into fully functional and
aesthetically pleasing pieces of architecture
and urbanity both inside and out.

later, now with both teams and other experts AHMM deemed necessary. By then results from research into history/context/systems/precedents would be in place, plus tests of one or two initial ideas. AKT II would be expected to have supporting studies ready, and ideas were thrashed through together without delay and founded on a 'trust of the other'; minor and major innovations were pulled out for the next session with the client's team. Communication of ideas was clear, sometimes highly manicured, but always sharp and inclusive. The pace and communication made – and still make – projects fun and exciting.

Continuing Professional Development and Teaching

Most projects start with a plan sketch, though a section is not going too far, but it is the plan that builds the architecture if any pattern exists. The White Collar Factory (Old Street Roundabout, London, 2017) is the project that unites the results of our years of collaborative work. I recall distinctly that to arrive at the now well-published 'key principles' we started with a material – reinforced concrete – and investigated how we could take it further. AHMM led an extensive piece of research to convince the client to bring to London a unique 'non-institutional' workspace with many attributes and permutations of a community. AHMM and the client were fascinated by French architect and designer Jean Prouvé, who famously said: 'If people understand there is no need to explain. If they don't there is no use explaining.'[1] The quote, possibly apocryphal, expresses the recognition that what makes great architecture and design is sometimes as unquantifiable as it is immediately apparent.

To me it is this quality of the spaces and building that persuaded AKT II to make White Collar our home. It is truly 'delightful and joyous',[2] with different depths of pleasure from the light, volumes, exposed concrete and lobbies that for us as occupants and engineers make it a very inspiring place in which to work.

Like many architects, AHMM have struggled with the trope of modern/postmodern architecture that embeds in its culture the directive that a façade ought to fit tightly around its building. They generate their buildings from the plan, and though I am tempted to refer to Robert Venturi's Duck/decorated shed dichotomy[3] to refer to each building, that would need another essay, as would the discussion of how the contemporary buildings of the future might be made.

AHMM,
White Collar Factory,
Old Street Roundabout,
London,
2017

The building is a result of AHMM's long-standing interest and research into creating pleasing and efficient contemporary workplaces that are also new pieces of public realm, where delight and conviviality are encouraged.

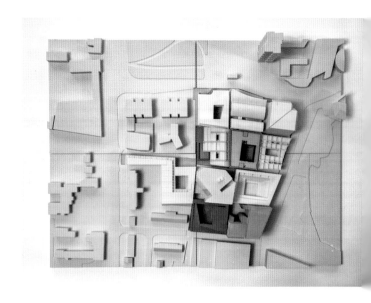

Composite student model,
Universal Building, Canada Water, London,
Harvard University
Graduate School of Design (GSD),
Cambridge, Massachusetts,
2020

Students who took part in Hanif Kara and Simon Allford's Harvard studio were asked to design a 'universal building' inspired by the Surrealist movement's 'exquisite corpse' game, in which a collection of words or images is collectively assembled, either by following set rules or with later participants not being able to see earlier portions. The building metamorphoses, accommodating mixed uses that change over time.

This mix of affordable keyworker and high-end apartments consists of three wings with brightly coloured outdoor 'sky rooms'. These punctuate the rough-sawn larch cladding, referencing the warehouse that previously functioned on the site.

Curiosity is the quality that sharpens critical practice beyond what we build, invigorates what we do, and reinforces the role our disciplines play in city-making and the value created by design

Simon, AHMM and I have always been interested in design education as part of our ongoing professional development. Curiosity is the quality that sharpens critical practice beyond what we build, invigorates what we do, and reinforces the role our disciplines play in city-making and the value created by design. In 2018 we were able to put this interest into practice by co-teaching a four-month Harvard University Graduate School of Design (GSD) studio, based in our studio at the White Collar Factory. The brief was to explore the idea of the 'universal building' at a site in Canada Water, London. The starting point was 'the exquisite corpse', the Surrealist discourse based on the collaborative folded-paper game described by the movement's leader André Breton: 'We had at our disposal – at last – an infallible means of sending the mind's critical mechanism away on vacation and fully releasing its metaphorical potentialities.'[4] As one would expect, the enquiry was inconclusive, but it was another chapter in the continuing process of questioning and investigation that lie at the heart of our practices.

One thing is sure: AHMM is a significant practice that has already had a big influence on architectural culture, particularly in the UK. They will become even more significant as time goes on. ᴆ

Notes
1. See www.artnet.com/artists/jean-prouv%C3%A9/.
2. From the author's speech on moving to the White Collar Factory, 2017.
3. Robert Venturi, Denise Scott Brown and Steven Izenour, *Learning from Las Vegas*, MIT Press (Cambridge, MA), 1972.
4. André Breton, 'The Exquisite Corpse, Its Exaltation' [1948], in André Breton, *Surrealism and Painting*, trans Simon Watson Taylor, MacDonald (London), 1972, p 289.

Morag Myerscough

Colourful Collaboration

Creating Joyous Ambiences

London-based artist and designer **Morag Myerscough** has a long history working in collaboration with AHMM, a story that dates back to the very beginnings of both studios. Myerscough specialises in colourful wayfinding super-graphics and place-making architectural interventions. Here she describes some of her work with the practice.

AHMM and Studio Myerscough,
Kentish Town Health Centre,
London,
2008

Airy spaces are enlivened with joyous,
free-form murals that bring scale
and bursts of colour to the interior.

My first encounter with AHMM was in the early 1990s. Fledgling architects did not have a voice at that time so Paul Monaghan, Simon Allford, Peter Morris and Jonathan Hall, with a group of young architects, had got together to make the Royal Institute of British Architects (RIBA) take notice of them and planned a series of exhibitions at the RIBA headquarters building – 'Under 50K', 'Rising Suns', 'Designing for Doctors', 'Continental Drift', 'The Unseen Hand'. I had just set up my first studio, Myerscough & Chipchase, and was eager to work on exciting projects. We were introduced to the group; they needed posters for their exhibitions, and we jumped at the chance. It was all of us helping each other and was my introduction to the world of architecture.

By the end of 1993 I had set up Studio Myerscough on my own. The same year *Design Week* magazine and the development and investment company British Land were running a competition to design a hoarding in the City of London, and AHMM and I decided to collaborate. It was our first large-scale collaboration. London streets were very controlled at the time – no colourful street art. Together we proposed a 65-metre (210-foot) 3D zigzag upper hoarding with the word 'FAMILIARITY'. The idea was to get people to think twice about the things they see every day and to rethink their surroundings.

Myerscough & Chipchase,
RIBA exhibition posters,
London,
1992-3

Morag Myerscough started her long
association with AHMM in the early 1990s.
She and her then business partner Jane
Chipchase produced numerous posters for
RIBA exhibitions featuring young architects.

We all look at something and acknowledge its presence, but when we consciously use our eyes to see, we start to be aware and begin to understand. One direction read 'FAMILIARITY', and the other direction was images of everyday objects commissioned by the photographer Trevor Key, who was known for his record covers for the rock band New Order and for using very bright single-colour backgrounds. The ground-level hoarding was a multicoloured Time Out-style guide to the neighbourhood to introduce the passer-by to the richness of the surrounding area that could be discovered in a lunchtime. We enlisted a very young Tom Dyckhoff who was a student in AHMM's unit at the Bartlett School of Architecture, University College London, to research and write all the content that would appear on the hoarding.

It is telling of what different times those were that there was backlash in the press, including one of the broadsheets saying that such a colourful piece of work was not suitable for the City of London and should be taken down.

AHMM and Studio Myerscough,
'FAMILIARITY' hoarding,
City of London,
1993

This creative use of a construction-site hoarding caused some
consternation in the City of London and in some elements
of the press, getting AHMM and Studio Myerscough noticed.

The Power of Narrative and Colour

From that moment on I think we could all see the power of narrative and colour in the urban environment.

It is hard for me to say why AHMM could see the value I brought to our collaboration. For me Paul Monaghan was visionary; he really saw that my involvement in their projects gave another vital layer. Instead of making a building that was just occupied by people, we wanted from the very beginning to make the best building for the occupants with the occupants. To make places rather than spaces. To find the narrative of the people and how to help build a better future with them and for them.

Colour was just one aspect of the work we did together. Our main aim was to understand what these buildings were aiming to achieve, and every project was very different.

With the refurbishment of London's Barbican Arts Centre (2006), I was involved from the pitch stage, and the initial documents coined the phrase 'Meet me by the blue bar'. Together with wayfinding design experts Cartlidge Levene, we had spent a long time trying to work out why the Barbican was so impossible to navigate, and it was partly because there were no identifiable landmarks within the building. Layers of alterations over time had confused things even more. So we went back to original interiors of the building and analysed what worked and what did not. We reinstated the orange for the auditorium and the red for the theatre, added a blue bar, and made the space much simpler, much more intuitive to navigate. Colour played a large part but it was more about understanding how the building could move forward. The whole project was about wayfinding, but it was not about adding: instead, it was about stripping back and using the building to make its own navigation.

AHMM, Studio Myerscough and Cartlidge Levene, Barbican Arts Centre refurbishment, City of London, 2006

Until 2006 the Barbican had been notoriously difficult to navigate for pedestrians. Colour was the key to creating successful wayfinding graphics.

AHMM and
Studio Myerscough,
Westminster Academy at
the Naim Dangoor Centre,
London,
2007

The school is animated by the
supergraphics created from a
variety of hues of green which
are used for interiors and
exterior. This makes for a playful,
welcoming and bright ambience.

For me, how colour is used in architecture is extremely important: it should have a reason for being there, and I feel strongly about how colours are produced. I worked with AHMM on the very early stages of the façade of the London high school Westminster Academy with AHMM Associate Director Susie Le Good. Green was settled on as the colour. This was the first school we had worked on together and it had a good build budget so the materials were not restricted. Glazed terracotta tiles were chosen, which are a wonderful material that stands the test of time, but most importantly the glaze responds to the light and the building colours change throughout the day. We could choose beautiful greens and we painstakingly looked at different hues of green to get the graduation we wanted to achieve absolutely right. The

building was completed in 2007 and it looks as vibrant now as the day it was built.

The collective vision for the school was to make the best school possible, to give the pupils the highest ambitions – if they wanted to be Prime Minister, there should be nothing stopping them. It was up to all of us to create environments that made this achievable for the students. The aim was to make places people were proud to be part of, where they could work together and thrive and have a collective feeling of belonging, so that without question they could become who they wanted to be.

Throughout the interior we hand-painted all the supergraphics again to get the colours exactly right: there is a big difference between hand-painting and vinyl graphics.

Morag Myerscough,
Atoll,
1 Finsbury Avenue,
London,
2019

The Atoll is a stand-alone
café structure, inspired by
Myerscough's memories of
being brought up in London and
childhood domesticity. Designed
in connection with AHMM's
refurbishment of this listed early
1980s office building, it brings the
feeling of abstracted historical
London forms into the space
and provides a focal point to the
common parts of the structure as
a whole, creating an enlivened
meeting place.

Pattern Workshops with the Community

I continued working on schools with AHMM – nine in total. Each posed its own unique set of problems to solve: there was absolutely no option for a 'one size fits all' approach. It was important that the schools had their own unique identities. At Waverley School in Birmingham (2013) I led pattern workshops with the students and they were brilliant, making intricate geometric patterns. I then made a piece of work incorporating all their patterns so all the students involved could see they were part of the mural in their own school. In Kingswood Academy, Hull (2012) I led word and pattern workshops with the wider community – to get them involved with the new school, to help make it become a community hub and to ensure people were not afraid or anxious about coming and interacting with it.

Burntwood School (2014), in the London borough of Wandsworth, was the last school we made together. The design was an incredibly close collaboration with AHMM and the school community. The school had a strong vision and it was for us to listen and then take it even further than they expected.

The school's starting point was the Bauhaus – not a bad one to choose. My knowledge of the Bauhaus had gone a bit rusty, so I did quite a lot of reading. Instead of responding directly to the Bauhaus I wanted to do my own take on it. I worked closely with AHMM and instead of naming the different buildings on the campus, we decided to allocate a colour to each, so they would be referred to as the blue/green/yellow building. The colour was built into the architecture in the form of a random triangular pattern of digitally printed tiles. We tested these colours for over a year to get them right. Inside each building the murals corresponded to that building's colour – again very importantly all hand-painted on the wall. That was until we got to the black building, where I brought all the colours together and made multicoloured hand-painted plywood installations. Throughout the whole of the project the triangle was the only geometric shape used.

I had read that Wassily Kandinsky described the triangle, square and circle as the dynamic triangle/yellow, static square/red and the serene circle/blue.

When I work with colour I do not use colour theory; I choose colours instinctively. It is really important to understand the space and to be able to read drawings and then visit the site as early as possible to understand scale, distances etc.

An Evolving Practice

Paul never restricted me. On more than one occasion I asked him whether he was sure we should be as bold as this. He would give me freedom, and that is down to trust, and when I am given the freedom it is absolutely when I give my best, but I think that is true of many of us.

The aim of the GPs who were set to practise at the new Kentish Town Health Centre (2008), also in London, was to provide a joyful place to visit – a place where people would feel comfortable, that would lessen their anxiety and would be different from any other healthcare centre. AHMM filled the space with natural light through a double-height space opening out onto a beautiful calm garden courtyard. Paul designed the building in a totally integrated way from the start, making a canvas for wall interventions. The intention for these was not as a layer on top but as part of the fabric of the building, all the elements working together to make a whole. The walls were filled with supersize merging coloured pictograms that travel along the corridors and rise up into the main space. The scale means they can be read as abstract colours, or if you want to look twice the pictograms will emerge. I watched a father with his small child using the walls to pass the time and point out what each pictogram was.

In the period since working on the schools, my practice has developed and moved direction. Now I mainly build large temporary structures. In September 2018 Paul Monaghan contacted me and said they had a project I might be interested in. It was to look at making a café in the centre of the atrium space of 1 Finsbury Avenue – a Grade II-listed, early 1980s office building in the City of London, originally designed by Peter Foggo of Arup Associates, that they were refurbishing. AHMM had designed a beautiful bold industrial space, black and white, ready to take something that was strong and vibrant. The building was moving from being a closed corporate space to an open public place for everyone to use. The prospect of this project filled me with immense excitement. It could not just be a café; it had to be a piece that connected directly to the rich history of London, that had a story, and to be honest it became my own story: growing up in a typical terraced house in Holloway, with a back yard, and the only open green spaces being parks. I wanted to bring this collective London domestic life inside the building. The colours needed to be rich and full of materiality and the planting to be luscious.

I have since heard Paul was shocked when he first saw it but was prepared for me to present the 'Atoll' to British Land. Now it is built and is a successful meeting point in their building. ⌂

Text © 2021 John Wiley & Sons Ltd. Images: pp 96–7 © Rob Parrish; pp 98(t), 99(t) © Morag Myerscough; pp 98(b), 99(b) © John Frederick Anderson; pp 100–03 photos Tim Soar.

AHMM,
Burntwood School,
Wandsworth, London,
2014

Studio Myerscough were involved in the interior and exterior wayfinding and interior treatments, creating a joyful, colourful, interesting and non-threatening ambience in which to learn.

Environmen From the In the Parame

Patrick Bellew

AHMM,
Tower Hamlets Civic Centre,
London,
due for completion 2021/2022

The historic Royal London Hospital reinvented as
the new Civic Centre in the heart of the borough's
Whitechapel community is wrapped by extensive
newbuild elements. The BIM model facilitated
the stitching together of the new with the old.

tal Design
tuitive to
tric

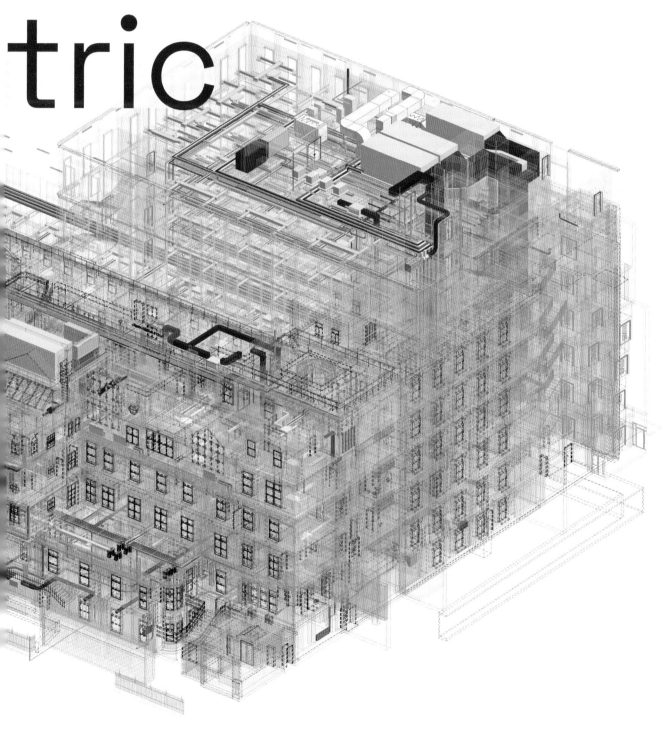

Founding Director of London's Atelier Ten environmental engineering consultants, **Patrick Bellew** lifts the lid on some of his firm's numerous interactions with AHMM and their continuing, joint aspirations to create greener, sustainable buildings that rejoice in bringing together science and art.

It seems like a small thing now, winning a design competition for a primary school, but it was a big moment for Ateliers One and Ten and the still-small team at AHMM at the time. It was 1996 and the Design Council and Essex County Council had run an open competition for a prototype model sustainable primary school to be built in the Garden Village of Notley Green. We were fledgling practices. AHMM founders Simon Allford, Jonathan Hall, Paul Monaghan and Peter Morris had their offices a stone's throw from ours and we were collaborating with the unit they were running at the Bartlett School of Architecture, University College London (UCL). It was a modest building with an appropriately modest budget, but it had big ambitions to be a game changer, and we all applied ourselves to the task with serious intent. We trooped out of the interview at the Design Council with the real feeling that everything had fallen into place and that we had a winning design. As it turned out, we had.

We had been developing ideas around the passive performance of buildings through our work together in the Bartlett unit, but with the competition came the opportunity to apply the thinking about issues of form, massing, daylighting, natural ventilation, biophilia and embodied carbon to make a replicable model for many schools around the county. As it turned out we only built one because of procurement rules, but what a great multi-award-winning school building it turned out to be.

AHMM,
Great Notley Primary School,
Essex, England,
1999

right: The twin goals of achieving simple natural cross-ventilation and balanced daylight in teaching spaces led to the roofscape at Great Notley. The triangular plan was very efficient for surface area and for simple effective ventilation with light from the sides and the north. The all-timber construction foresaw many of today's embodied carbon conversations.

AHMM,
Jubilee Primary School,
Lambeth, London,
2002

The school has a tripartite
organisation manifested in three
buildings that cosset outside
playing and sporting spaces.

Rediscovering Environmental Design Drivers

The idea of using environmental forces as a design driver in architecture is as old as architecture itself, but at the time the conversations seemed to represent something of a process of rediscovery. We talked about how mainstream architecture had disengaged from taking responsibility for the wider environment through the 20th century. As AHMM developed their own architectural style and language it was clear that consideration for the environment was going to play a big part.

We all felt that the profession could do better, and our discourse was around making the architecture do the heavy lifting and leaving the services to do the minimum of work; pretty obvious really, but still not common in practice at that time. From the outset we brought structure and materials as well as environmental performance to the heart of the process. Most of all, the AHMM team understood the power of a strong narrative around the issue of environmental design and the necessity of integrating it into their projects, instead of it being an addition that could be value-engineered out. Looking back, I realise how much myself and my colleagues at Atelier Ten have been influenced in our work through their strong grasp of narrative, and the power of graphics, to break down and convey complex ideas.

Schools and the Stirling Prize

The conversations continued when we were appointed together to work on the Jubilee Primary School in Tulse Hill, South London, which completed in 2002. Here the two-storey configuration included vertical lightwells linked to mini wind-towers at the back of each of the classrooms to provide natural cross-ventilation and additional daylight to reduce brightness contrast in the space. A succession of school collaborations followed through the nineties and noughties. For all the attention and innovation that AHMM have lavished on educational projects since they began in practice together it seemed very appropriate that they should win the Stirling Prize in 2015 for a quite exceptional one: Burntwood School in the London borough of Wandsworth. Not one of our collaborations, but nonetheless familiar in its handling of light, air and materiality.

As well as the schools, we worked in that period on a wider range of building types including the award-winning Walsall Bus Station in the West Midlands (2000), the Battleship Building in Paddington, London, for Monsoon (2001), and by the late noughties projects at Barking Central (2010) and the North London Hospice (2012). The attention to detail and the care given to the sectioning and fenestration that brings extravagant daylight and airiness into the heart of the quite modest hospice project showed that even though the practice had grown to a significant size, there remained a keen enjoyment of well-executed detail.

Civic Design

A more recent competition win together was for a new Civic Centre for the London Borough of Tower Hamlets on the site of the Royal London Hospital on Whitechapel Road (due for completion 2021/2022). The careful conversion of 'London's oldest hospital' building into a new front door for the borough includes extensive offices and civic facilities in new structures that wrap around and engage with the historic fabric. A very challenging project on many levels, it required clear thinking, patience and determination in equal measure, and the bench depth that is one of AHMM's great strengths was very much

AHMM,
Google Hyderabad,
India,
2017–

A significant new building in the hot and humid environment of Hyderabad. With limited infrastructure availability and reliability, the design focused on minimising energy demands through the passive design, very efficient systems and deployment of extensive solar collection.

in evidence. This was also our first foray together into the world of building information modelling (BIM) at a large scale, and we learned a lot about the challenges of stitching the old and new together in this medium.

Working with Google

Today we are working together on buildings at a much larger scale. With scale comes complexity and multiplied risk, but also opportunity for a deeper numerical exploration of the many variables in play in the modern high-performance building. AHMM have a long relationship with Google, and in 2017 secured the commission for a very large technical building for them in Hyderabad, India. This presented us with a relatively rare opportunity to work together on an international project in a much more climatically challenging environment than the UK, and with limited infrastructure and resources. Among the many design studies, we together dived deep into the evaluation of façade performance. With a deep plan-form, daylight is at a premium, but the levels of solar energy are intense and need to be excluded. We looked to cues from vernacular architecture to develop and parametrically test options, including a jali screen, optimised for daylight.

AHMM,
Belgrove House,
King's Cross,
London,
due for completion 2024

above: The demolition and redevelopment of a site on Euston Road to create a state-of-the-art laboratory and office building with high sustainability ambitions and industry-leading low-carbon emissions. The development is an expansion to London's Knowledge Quarter and will offer the community employment opportunities and new amenities at street level.

AHMM,
115–123 Houndsditch,
London,
due for completion 2024

right: This proposed new commercial building in the City of London for Brockton Everlast has been subjected to an exceptional amount of analysis of the embodied carbon associated with different configurations of core and structure. The learning journey never ends in the world of environmental architecture, and now better data and ever-deeper analysis is taking design optimisation and decision-making to a new level.

These projects are representative of a new and more technical era where ideas are tested to a much higher level of detail than was possible a few years ago

Embodied Carbon Takes Centre Stage

Among our current collaborations is a new office building at 115–123 Houndsditch in the City of London for Brockton Capital. We are in a moment where the changed backdrop of corporate social responsibility, legislation and benchmarking around sustainability in the face of the climate crisis has led to a significant shift in market attitude. The decarbonisation of the UK's national electricity grid has also fundamentally changed the ground rules and realigned priorities. As a result, the concept design for this project is being subjected to an extraordinary amount of analysis in a concerted effort across the team to optimise massing, form, column grid, fenestration and many other variables with a view to achieving the very demanding targets recommended by the Royal Institute of British Architects (RIBA) and London Energy Transport Initiative (LETI). The process has been characterised by the AHMM teams' willingness to revisit and dig ever deeper into the impacts of designing for daylight, mixed-mode ventilation and changing grids in pursuit of lower emissions. It remains a work in progress, but is due for completion in 2024.

Similar conversations are being played out regarding a new office and medical science building, Belgrove House in King's Cross (2024), where planning for medical laboratories adds a new layer of complexity to the design discussions and narrative.

These projects are representative of a new and more technical era where ideas are tested to a much higher level of detail than was possible a few years ago. Numbers are great, but architecture is about so much more, and over the years Allford, Hall, Monaghan and Morris have shown themselves to be very adept at bridging art and science in a professional, collaborative, friendly but detailed way.

Long may it continue. ∆

Joe Morris

A Symbiotic Relationship

Reminiscences of the Family

Morris+Company and AHMM,
Royal Street,
Lambeth, London,
2019-

Competition-winning study model for a plot in an
emerging MedTech regeneration scheme in South
London, in collaboration with Copenhagen-based
architecture and urban planning practice Cobe.
Morris+Company's involvement builds on the working
principles of open engagement and collaboration
with AHMM and a number of other prolific architects,
engineers and designers.

Architect **Joe Morris** was a student of Simon
Allford and Paul Monaghan's design unit at
the Bartlett School of Architecture, University
College London. After graduation he joined
the still-small practice and subsequently rose
through the ranks before leaving to form
his own architectural firm, Morris+Company,
which has worked with AHMM on some large
urban schemes.

In the mid-1990s, Diploma Unit 10 of the Bartlett School of Architecture, University College London (UCL) seemed unique. Its leaders were actual practising architects, with actual building projects, of emerging note. It was not a unit vested in theoretical meandering, but one that sought to reflect directly upon the connections between academia and practice. Cut to the interview. A nervous student. Two grey-suit-wearing professors, a half-empty box of Silk Cut on a small table and an ashtray already straining.

On the left, Simon Allford, legs crossed and sporting a mop of thick curly hair; and to the right, Paul Monaghan, a little more dishevelled, drawing deeply on the final embers of a cigarette. Our discussion direct and to the point – character traits of both Simon and Paul. They made the case for their unit and I made the case for my ambitions. Within a short period we had reached consensus and I joined their unit.

As far as the rest of the story goes, this one encounter almost 30 years ago has done more to shape the course of my career than any other meeting before or after, and has seen my personal dynamic grow from student, to apprentice, to trusted employee, to friend and currently as collaborator.

The Big, Wide World

In July 1996, a month after the completion of my Diploma, I was invited to join AHMM for a quick hit to build a model for a couple of weeks. Eight years later I was still there. This period turned me from a student, who in the words of Simon 'knew nothing about architecture', into an architect equipped with a range of business and design skills that enabled me to start my own practice in 2004. Sixteen years later, Morris+Company has grown to over 50 team members, with studios in London and Copenhagen. In the meantime, AHMM has emerged as one of the leading UK practices of a generation, its size outgrowing almost all others, and with offices in London, Bristol and Oklahoma.

When I joined, AHMM was a very different place, just 11-strong including the partners. A far cry from today, with a studio of around 500. The entire practice then occupied a small first-floor studio space in a cluster of warehouses on Old Street known as Moreland Buildings, serendipitously resulting in the focus for my first building project for client Derwent London, which lasted some four years. The present-day practice now occupies several blocks of these same buildings, including its own roof extension replete with flying bridges that link it all together.

The studio then was around 280 square metres (3,000 square feet) in size, with a small kitchenette to the right-hand side of the front door, which also housed a fax machine, and the smaller of two meeting spaces to the left. The main space saw two rows of large parallel-motion adjustable drawing-boards running along the outer edge of the rectangular-shaped space with larger breakout tables in the centre. To the far-left-hand side of the office, a dark multifunction space, which was the practice coat-room, storage space, archive and materials library. To the far right, the main meeting-room with its large sliding door. By today's standards, the space was conspicuous for the absence of computer hardware. It was also heavy with the fug of cigarette smoke, the accompaniment to every design review, and the manifestation of the stresses and strains of the fledgling character of the practice.

All-for-One and One Family

The compact roots of the practice facilitated an all-for-one spirit with design reviews at times encompassing the entire office. As time passed, and projects increased in scale and complexity, Allford and Monaghan began spearheading large and distinct teams framed by the multiple projects each partner was leading. Simultaneously, Peter Morris morphed into the practice management role, a natural evolution of his own character traits, and one that is now a monumental task. And of course, the enigmatic Jonathan Hall, a closet turf accountant, naturally migrated to lead every legal, financial and contractual agreement of every project.

Reflecting on AHMM's past, I recall a steady stream of many other architects, designers and figureheads who would flow in and out of the studio spaces with increasing regularity over the years. Characters who were not staff. Characters you would glance passing along the rows of desks before disappearing into meeting rooms, doors closed, plots and schemes being hatched. Characters of some note: Cedric Price, Roger Zogolovitch, Jeremy Melvin, Lee Mallett, Susanne Isa, Simon Herron, Morag Myerscough and Azhar Azhar to name but a few, alongside engineers and specialists too many to name, many of whom I now class as personal friends and collaborators. Perhaps I had not quite realised the power of the network and the ambition to work with those whom you hold in high esteem. But needless to say, my methods in practice follow a similar pattern, whereby the collaboration is more valuable than the sum of its parts.

Matrix of study options for the Television Centre. Optioneering has been an integral component of the approach to Morris+Company's work – a method reflective of AHMM's own practice of architecture.

Morris+Company and AHMM,
Television Centre,
White City, London,
2018

The Morris+Company team worked closely and
collaboratively with AHMM's team to evolve a
scheme that captured the spirit of the Television
Centre site – one that draws the motif of the
question mark through many of the buildings.

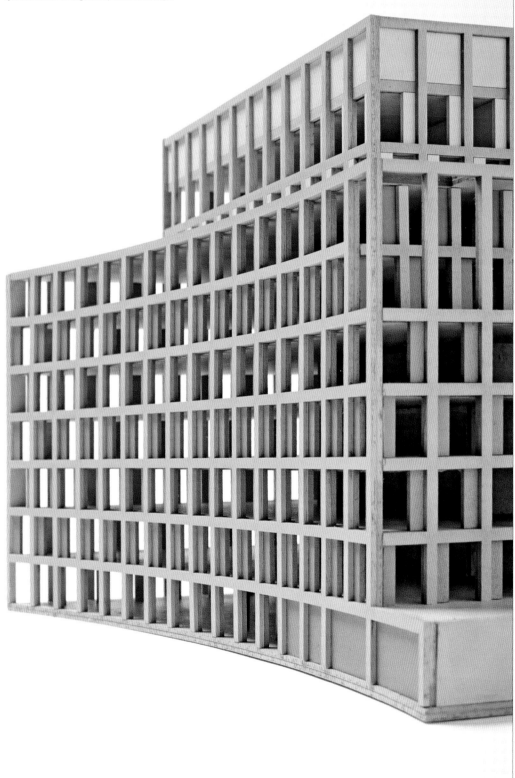

Morris+Company and AHMM,
Blossom Street,
Spitalfields,
London,
due for completion 2022

The sense of family extends downwards beyond the partner team to include many significantly talented people whom Morris+Company has collaborated with directly on a raft of projects that have been important for the practice, including Blossom Street in London's Spitalfields

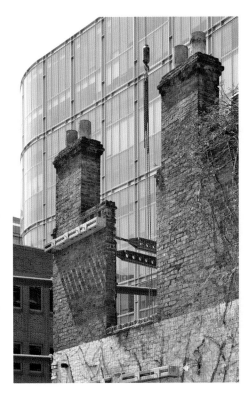

above left and right: A complex stitching of new buildings into a piece of historic city fabric, the build process for Blossom Street requires fastidious attention to detail, and care. The project involves equal measures of newbuild, rebuild, retrofit and extension.

left: The Blossom Street project has many divergent and complex issues. Morris+Company's involvement required continuous evolution, developed through a range of model-making techniques that were used as the basis for debate.

AHMM in some ways has always been my family, the partners each a father figure and a mentor to the four corners of my professional being. This band of four, my very own pop-poster-pinups, have been invaluable in my own evolution – a backdrop against which my own organisation has emerged, a lens through which to observe the growing value of the culture of practice, and a benchmark of professionalism and respect.

And, of course, the sense of family extends downwards beyond the partner team to include many significantly talented people whom Morris+Company has collaborated with directly on a raft of projects that have been important for the practice, including Blossom Street in London's Spitalfields for British Land (due for completion in 2022), and Television Centre at White City (2018) for Stanhope. It is important to note that each project has led to further opportunities and working relationships, which is the true spirit of collaboration.

When AHMM won the Stirling Prize in 2015 for its adaptation and transformation of Burntwood School, a 1950s Modernist campus in South-West London, I had already been distant from the practice with my own burdens for more than a decade. But the pervading essence of family that beats to the tune of hundreds of hearts is astonishing. I think everyone still working there, or who had passed through the practice previously, at that moment felt an immense sense of collective pride and reason to rejoice. The announcement of the prize normatively on a Thursday, I recall a Stirling Prize party at Paul's house the following Saturday, the atmosphere raucous, infectious, glorious, celebratory and mutual, and the celebrations inclusive, shared, accommodating and human. ⌂

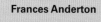
Frances Anderton

The New Establishment

AHMM,
Richmond House,
Northern Estate,
Westminster, London,
due for completion 2025

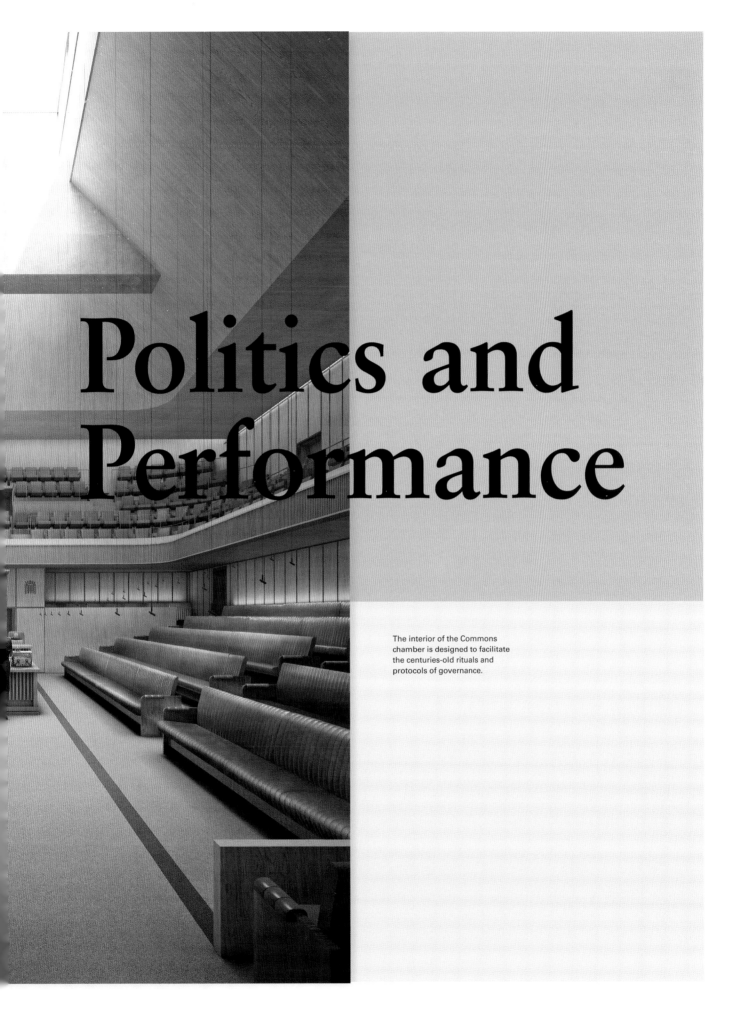

Politics and Performance

The interior of the Commons chamber is designed to facilitate the centuries-old rituals and protocols of governance.

Frances Anderton, an old friend of AHMM, is a Los Angeles-based curator, writer and broadcaster on design and architecture. Here she remembers their student bar conversations in London 30 years ago and describes two of the practice's most prestigious contemporary buildings: the Soho Place offices/theatre at Tottenham Court Road, and Richmond House for the temporary relocation of the House of Commons.

It has been said that a sure sign you are getting old is when your mates from college are running the country. And that is the case with Simon Allford, Paul Monaghan, Jonathan Hall and Peter Morris. One minute I was sharing laughs with them over a drink at the makeshift foyer bar at the Bartlett School of Architecture, University College London (UCL). The next minute, as in 30 years later, the former 'Bartlett Boys' are at the epicentre of the establishment, designing two buildings that are foundational to British culture and politics: a new West End theatre and a temporary home for the House of Commons while the Palace of Westminster, home to the Houses of Parliament, is renovated.

In some ways these projects are connected. Each is the outcome of navigating highly complex site demands and multiple stakeholders. Each is about giving form to a ritualised experience that has been honed over hundreds of years: the conduct of Parliament, the performance of a play. In a sense, both are theatre. Each is a repository for an intensively social experience, dependent for effect on human proximity in very tight space. (It is, of course, odd to be writing about this at the very time such closeness is banned during the COVID-19 pandemic.) Each takes a type of space known for dark, ornate interiors and lets in more light, literally. And each plays to strengths of AHMM that one might say are very British (notwithstanding the firm's satellite in Oklahoma and their evident love of American Modernists like Louis Kahn, Gordon Bunshaft and the transplant Mies van der Rohe): pragmatism, empiricism, craft, competence, a lack of dogma and an ability to find architectural power in compromise.

Governance

Let us start with the Parliament project, under the direction of Paul Monaghan. It involves creating a temporary House of Commons while the crumbling and fire-prone Palace of Westminster is restored. Six hundred and fifty MPs and members of the House of Lords will be 'decanted' in 2025 from their Gothic Revival bottle designed by Charles Barry and Augustus Pugin into two nearby sites. The Lords will go to the Queen Elizabeth II Conference Centre, and the Commons next door to the Northern Estate, a block of buildings that includes Norman Shaw North and South, Portcullis House by Hopkins Architects, and Richmond House, designed by the late Sir William Whitfield. New Scotland Yard by AHMM sits on the edge of the Northern Estate.

In collaboration with the firm BDP, who are masterplanning the Northern Estate and refurbishing several of the structures, AHMM propose to demolish the rear two-thirds of Whitfield's Richmond House, which does not meet today's spatial, servicing and security needs, and replace it with a new temporary Commons chamber and various operations of Parliament, from members' offices to the tea room. They will landscape Canon Row and the service alleys crisscrossing the block to create a more inviting public realm while wrapping the parliamentary complex in a tall fence as well as layers of invisible security.

AHMM garnered this project via a framework process following their successful work on the New Scotland Yard

AHMM,
Richmond House,
Northern Estate,
Westminster, London,
due for completion 2025

Richmond House will temporarily accommodate the House of Commons and its associated office space while the Victorian Gothic Houses of Parliament are refurbished. The new building is punctuated with light.

There is much that is fascinating about the project, but especially those aspects that enshrine hundreds of years of ritualised performance, albeit in clean modern dress

The whole complex of Richmond House carefully integrates itself into and around William Whitfield's 1984 existing frontage on Whitehall.

building. What started out as a renovation job at the Northern Estate has morphed into a project that has put them in the crosshairs of public-spending watchdogs as well as some preservationists.

There is much that is fascinating about the project, but especially those aspects that enshrine hundreds of years of ritualised performance, albeit in clean modern dress. In the temporary Commons chamber, the architects were not permitted to change its essential form because the 'atmosphere is vital', says Monaghan. For hundreds of years seats have been arranged in long, close rows so members can be packed in for lively debate. They can all see the Speaker, who is positioned to overlook everyone, and leaders of opposing parties sit 'two swords' length' across from each other – just enough to stop the rabble in Parliament from poking each other's eyes out. The closeness of seats prescribed over time does not work, however, for today's needs, such as wheelchair access, so the architects have loosened up the spacing between seating, making it 'gentler'.

Notwithstanding the connection to past precedent, today's MPs are 'incredibly digital', points out Monaghan. 'Everything's on Twitter. Everyone's just looking at devices. And of course, just like when we were doing Scotland Yard, the building will be on television every day.'

So the building as backdrop matters. And this is where a dialogue with the Whitfield structure enters in. The Grade II* listed Richmond House, aka 79 Whitehall, was built to house the Department of Health and Social Security, and completed in 1987. That time period was both peak-IRA and peak-Postmodernism, so the building is both fortress and cake, with decorative oriel windows and stone-and-red-brick banding echoing Norman Shaw North (the former New Scotland Yard building) opposite.

Some critics have been fighting the demolition of Richmond House on architectural and public-spending grounds. AHMM have responded to cost complaints with concepts for legacy use of the new building when Parliament has returned to the Palace of Westminster. Architecturally they offer a homage: a generous stair echoing the Whitfield stair tower and, says Monaghan, 'I suppose our big idea about Whitfield – given we're taking his building down – is the oriel windows'. They propose turning the back of Whitfield's façade with its oriel windows into the money shot: it will become the interior wall of the Central Lobby of the House of Commons and get nonstop television coverage.

While façades have a modern aesthetic, they take clues from Whitfield's existing frontage, such as the masonry banding.

Playing in the West End

In the city's West End, Simon Allford and his team have designed a pair of sleek office buildings with ground-floor retail buildings that straddle a new civic plaza leading past St Patrick's Church to Soho Square. Called Soho Place, and due for completion in 2022, the development is opposite Centrepoint at the intersection of Oxford Street, Tottenham Court Road and Charing Cross Road. The southern building sits on the site of the once grotty but fun London Astoria live music venue, and there is a twist; it contains an arthouse performance space that will be the first new West End theatre in 50 years. The entire complex sits above the Tottenham Court Road Crossrail station where thousands of passengers will board trains that will whizz them to Heathrow Airport in 17 minutes.

Like the Richmond House renovation, the project is a Rubik's cube of architectural and stakeholder complexity that took two decades to wrestle into reality. It brought together Nimax Theatres owner Nica Burns, developers Derwent, who have partnered many times with AHMM, London Transport and the City of Westminster in a private and public deal fusing air rights and personal and artistic ambition. 'This is built out of infrastructure,' says Allford. That is because in normal circumstances they would never have been allowed to demolish the buildings. To that was added 'an extraordinary kind of piece of London financial magic that is allowed. So I think it's that idea of complexity, practicality, and the everyday and the imaginary coming together.'

The project is an extraordinary feat of engineering, by Arup. 'There is a point in the construction called the eye of the needle,' explains Allford. The trains go in 'within 200 millimetres [8 inches] of the existing Tottenham Court Road station. And we are building a theatre that must achieve better than NR [noise rating] 25, which is really super demanding. But it's next to a box that's generating three jet engines' worth of noise and vibrates every time a train comes in. As a result we can't have a normal design.'

The four-storey theatre is a box within a box on anti-vibration mounts above the subterranean Crossrail structure. Allford continues: 'It has a technical gallery running alongside, and within is a lift and stairs to offices above. The main palazzo-like office opposite and to the north also sits over the stations, stabilised by a cantilevered, vertical steel "bridge" that acts as its core. This is clad in glass to become a three-dimensional lightwell with lifts and stairs within – a kinetic vertical promenade.'

Kinesis and light are hallmarks of the theatre project, which is intended to have a lantern-like effect. Through its glass façade, passers-by will see bodies moving within behind its 3-millimetre thin Covelano limestone (itself encapsulated in glass) balconies and stairs. They will also see a sprinkling of stars on the ceilings, which Allford describes as 'constellations cast into the acoustic wrap of the theatre box'.

Such dashes of glitz and glamour are a must the team has embraced to keep Nica Burns on board. Burns is a powerhouse in the West End and owns, with her Nimax co-founder Max Weitzenhoffer, the Apollo, Duchess, Garrick, Lyric, Palace and Vaudeville theatres. None of these are see-through or remotely Modernist buildings. 'Modern theatres in Nica's view have all failed,' says Allford: 'They may have

AHMM,
Soho Place,
London,
due for completion 2022

above: The site is in close proximity to what will be a major new transport hub at Tottenham Court Road serving Crossrail's new 117-kilometre (73-mile) railway line linking East and West London. It included the old Astoria live music venue, which until the 1980s was a theatre; Westminster Council permitted this to be demolished only if another performance space were built somewhere on the site to replace it.

The four-storey theatre is a box within a box on anti-vibration mounts above the subterranean Crossrail structure

right: Neither developers Derwent nor AHMM had ever aspired to build a theatre, nor had they worked with theatre people, and it became clear that they needed a knowledgeable client. The project was too small to be interesting for London's four large subsidised theatre companies, so the independent Nimax Theatres group became the client.

It is in the heart of London. 'It is woven into the infrastructure and fabric of the city. So it's a giant Swiss watch – with all the associated complexity,' says Allford

architectural integrity, but they have no glamour.' So the challenge for AHMM was in figuring out how to deliver a building true to their architectural preoccupations, but with the secret sauce and special feeling of a Victorian London theatre like the Garrick.

In place of a horseshoe-shaped theatre with red velvet, gilt and ornamental mouldings is a flexible space that can take on seven different configurations, but exudes a richness through its 'dark indigo interior with golden-timber cladding'. In place of wood-panelled bars are 'crush bars', or 'tiny little intimate linear rooms' that are only 2.4 metres (7 feet) high. They are visible from the street where the drinkers become the actors framed between the mullions, and behind the Covelano limestone panels which provide places to lean, look and to be observed. For people who know Allford's love of the mid-century work of Skidmore, Owings & Merrill (SOM), they will see in this edifice a marriage of the Manufacturers Trust Company bank building in Manhattan and the Beinecke Rare Book and Manuscript Library at Yale University. But it is in the heart of London. 'It is woven into the infrastructure and fabric of the city. So it's a giant Swiss watch – with all the associated complexity,' says Allford.

The gestation of the theatre project was not all plain sailing. 'Nica and I didn't get on for two years,' recalls Allford. 'She thought I was a terrible man who couldn't stand theatre or her. I thought she was a prima donna. But she took me for a drink, we started again and she, Derwent and I have built up an incredibly strong friendship built on trust and shared ambition, and commitment to achieving the near impossible.'

A Drink with the 'Boys'

If AHMM are the same as they were 30 years ago, they are still the 'boys' you will want to have drinks with in one of those tiny crush bars in the new Nimax theatre. They are fun and unpretentious, and their work is unpretentious too. It has a firm voice, but not one that aims for loud self-expression or for an ironic take on a project, as you might find from some architects tasked with designing an institution steeped in tradition. 'We're not arrogant by nature,' says Monaghan. 'We're collaborative, and clients like us because we listen to them and interpret their work.'

It is worth noting that AHMM did not have the luxury of being arrogant. They launched their firm in 1989 at the start of a deep building recession. Like many contemporaries, they wandered in the professional wilderness for several years. By 1997, recalls Monaghan, 'I'd been earning £10,000 a year for five years. We were desperate by the late 1990s, and so every opportunity we remembered how bad it had been, and we went for it. And that drive has continued in our firm at every level. We're always saying we've got to do better, we've got to keep going.'

They are keeping on going, maybe into another bastion of the British establishment. At the time of writing, Allford has been elected as the next President of the RIBA. Monaghan, about to embark on building the temporary House of Commons next door to his firm's New Scotland Yard, reflects on where their careers have brought them: 'It is weird to be doing this building … and Simon becoming the RIBA President. Yeah, we have become the establishment.' ⌀

opposite top: Crossrail's massive subterranean civil engineering works included new passageways, a new entrance, a new transport hub connecting the new Elizabeth Line and the existing Northern London Underground lines, ventilation shafts with fans working to capacity, fire exits, and other services. These brought with them problems of noise and vibration and determined many of the design choices.

opposite bottom: The façade is glazed, allowing the building to be visually peopled both day and night as audiences gravitate towards the windows to have their drinks. Wide, plain cream-coloured-stone bands at floor level prevent upskirting and hide objects on the floor. A public piazza and cafe provide places for the public to meet and linger.

All quotes from Paul Monaghan and Simon Allford are from email correspondence and a conference call with the author in June 2020.

A Word from
AD Editor Neil Spiller

Old Buildings, New Architecture
Richard Griffiths Architects

**Richard Griffiths Architects,
Lambeth Palace,
London,
1999**

The careful juxtaposition of
new forms and materials
enlivens and rejuvenates this
courtyard within the official
London residence of the
Archbishop of Canterbury.

In all of its work, Richard Griffiths architects remains true to the creation of a timeless architecture, in which style derives from materials, use and construction rather than from the whims of fashion.

— Richard Griffiths Architects[1]

Old buildings are a fecund breeding ground for new architectural possibilities, an opportunity for contemporary architects to make another useful layer on the palimpsests of their history. London architect Richard Griffiths has spent most of his architectural career modifying, maintaining and rejuvenating them for the modern world. He sees such buildings as great living assets to the city, not simply something to be preserved in aspic as the world passes by: 'Old buildings also embody the attributes of age and of memory, and the architect who works with old buildings has the challenge of understanding their history and significance, of engaging with all the historic layers that are already present and of adding a new architectural layer.'[2]

Cambridge and London Epiphany
Griffiths went up to Cambridge originally to study engineering, but in 1974 switched to architecture, 'always with the view that I wanted to work at the interface between old and new'.[3] His great revelation came during a tutorial with the inspiring Dalibor Vesely about a mixed-use site in London's Kentish Town. One of Griffiths's most treasured possessions is Vesely's sketch from that day: 'His pencil never stopped moving, and its faint traces conjured up infinite possibilities in defiance of the determinism of the Modern Movement.'[4]

After graduation, Griffiths worked in Cambridge and London for various firms until in 1986 he finally arrived at Julian Harrap's practice where his enduring love of East London and its often derelict architectural treasures was nurtured: 'Having cut his teeth on rebuilding the houses in Spitalfields saved by Dan Cruickshank and Mark Girouard and others following the battle of Elder Street, Julian had become the pre-eminent architect working on historic buildings in East London.'[5] It is also at this point that Griffiths became involved in local societies and preservation trusts, not just using his architectural skills, but also being proactive in securing the protection of old buildings.

Griffiths and his firm, Richard Griffiths Architects (established in 1993), have a long history of this architectural palimpsestual overwriting. Their work includes such prestigious commissions as the repairs, refurbishments and upgrades to Southwark Cathedral (1997–2014), the Archbishop of Canterbury's residence Lambeth Palace (1999) and the Garrick Club (2004) in London, and Exeter College, Oxford (2013) to name but a few examples of their extensive experience. They have worked on historic houses, churches and cathedrals, and barn typologies, created newbuilds in historic contexts, developed new programmes for old buildings and designed historic gardens and landscapes; in short, they have worked on all aspects of the conservation and regeneration of old buildings being renewed for our time.

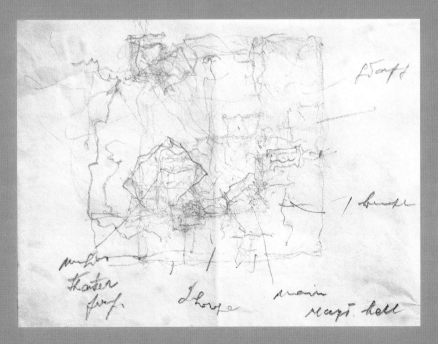

**Dalibor Vesely,
Sketch,
concert hall, apartments,
a genetic research
laboratory and a monastery,
Kentish Town, London,
1979**

A sketch drawn by Vesely while tutoring a young Richard Griffiths, evoking possibilities for urban development around a communal garden at the centre of each urban block.

Mending Broken Buildings

Since 2017, Richard Griffiths Architects have been collaborating with AHMM on the former Royal London Hospital on Whitechapel Road in the city's East End, augmenting and converting it into a new Civic Centre for the London Borough of Tower Hamlets. The hospital was founded in 1751 and has undergone much alteration as it attempted to keep pace with medical technology and innovation over the centuries. It has now been superseded by a newbuild, adjacent hospital. Working in any part of Central London is difficult at the best of times; the hospital, for example, was Grade II listed in 1973, and it has therefore been necessary to adhere to many development frameworks, and at the same time respecting the hospital's central position within one of the borough's conservation areas.

The objectives for the development were very clear. It should provide an ideal new public use for the building, contribute to the urban regeneration of Whitechapel and Tower Hamlets, restore and enhance the architecturally significant parts of the site, and be a unique combination of the best of the old and new. It also needed to contribute to the legibility of its immediate urban fabric, facilitating connecting vistas, aiding wayfinding and enhancing the public realm. Above all the building was to be an architectural catalyst to create a sustainable future for the area in terms of economic, social and environmental factors.

AHMM,
Tower Hamlets Civic Centre,
London,
2021

below: As with the interior, the new additions complement the existing and refurbished. Modern and traditional materials work in sympathetic harmony. The new complex of buildings consolidates wayfinding with urban vistas and will bring a vitality and commercial opportunities to the area.

A full-height atrium links the former hospital with the new buildings, the contrast between old and new creating a pleasing juxtaposition. Richard Griffith Architects' involvement was in compiling the Heritage Impact Assessment document.

The entrance is cut and defined by lowering the approach so that one can slip into the building underneath the historic façade.

At an initial visit to the site with AHMM, and to his joy and surprise, Griffiths discovered that the original 23-bay Georgian hospital building of the 1750s still mostly survived, hidden under all manner of subsequent architectural additions. The borough had commissioned a feasibility study that advocated the demolition of the rear half of the Georgian building. To avoid destroying it, writes Griffiths, 'We therefore helped to devise an alternative approach … [the Georgian Hospital] separated from a new Z-shaped new building by a full-height glazed atrium revealing the repaired original rear elevation.'[6] Using this idea, the team was able to maintain the Georgian building, utilising its cellular planning, repairing it and creating meeting and conference rooms.

So a design concept was hatched that architecturally honoured and responded to the varying architectural characters of some of the historical additions and alterations spanning 1757 to 1906; for example, the Arts and Crafts double-height operating theatres will be reused to contribute varied spatial opportunities to foster different uses as well as create a changing choreography of spatial experiences as one travels through the building. Combined with the newbuild aspects of the proposal, this will provide the Civic Centre with all manner of modern and historical interiors that can host contemporary functions.

The architectural definition of the new Civic Centre's entrance presented a particular challenge. Cutting a hole in the historical wing, out of scale with the Victorian space and façade rhythms, was architecturally problematic. The solution is maverick, yet sensitively successful. 'The external ground is lowered, instead, and a new wide glazed entrance made below. This gives access to the whole of the ground floor via steps and gentle ramps,'[7] writes Griffiths.

Continuity over Time

A lengthy career working on buildings of a variety of periods and styles has given Griffiths a detailed understanding of the UK's unique and long architectural history – there are always new things to learn, in terms of both construction and theory. His path has intersected with many architects and master-craftsmen often lost in the mists of time, and others fading into the dusk as contemporary architects and students continue on their solipsistic way, sometimes with a poor understanding and respect for architectural history before the 20th century. Griffiths's journey has been different, and has brought him into visceral architectural contact with many from the past: in London, greats such as Nicholas Hawksmoor and Albert Richardson (St Alfege Church, Greenwich), George Gilbert Scott (St Pancras Renaissance Hotel) and Charles Barry (Royal London Hospital, Whitechapel), as well as landscape designer Capability Brown, but equally those who deserve to be remembered, such as Victorians TG Jackson (Brighton College, East Sussex) and Elijah Hoole (Toynbee Hall, Whitechapel), and Edwardians Lanchester & Rickards (Methodist Central Hall, Westminster).

Richard Griffiths Architects, Extension of St Paul's Church, Hammersmith, London, 2005

opposite top: A highly sensitive addition to the neo-Gothic church rationalising its accommodation for a new century. The interior of the atrium, which conjoins the old and new, opens to the former baptistery of the church through three sets of glazed oak doors.

AHMM, Tower Hamlets Civic Centre, London, 2021

opposite bottom: The Council Chamber is unashamedly modern, but has a quiet, calming interior at once honorific yet also democratic.

He rejoices in the opportunities that designing with old buildings gives him to work with beautiful natural materials – stone, brick, oak, lead, wrought iron, brass and gold leaf. The combination of strict listed-building consents and the financial possibilities that successful bidding for historic building grants, often mean designing with quality raw materials and time-intensive quality craftsmanship. Such architecture can also escape the more severe quotidian cutbacks of contemporary 'value engineering' so prevalent in newbuild schemes.

Griffiths thinks and designs with a conception of the simultaneity of past, present and future. Firstly, designing new layers of old buildings raises his chances of having worked on a building that may still be existent in 500 years' time. The thought of this possibility gives him a heady sense of wellbeing. Also, most of his practice's work is on buildings in public ownership, and he gleans immense pleasure from watching people use and appreciate them: 'This is the richest reward for our work, whether attending evensong at Southwark or at St Albans Abbey, helping others to discover the fascination of Sutton House, or watching the crowds at Clissold House on a sunny weekend.'[8]

For Griffiths, his work is one of a continuum, a spectrum of preservation, rehabilitation and restoration, and he does not flinch from facsimile reconstruction. His experience has given him a thoughtful and realistic approach to the deeply worrying moral question raised when a great building is destroyed, for example by fire, as at the Mackintosh Building at the Glasgow School of Art in Scotland (2018), or Notre-Dame Cathedral in Paris (2019). Most Modernist architects get themselves into contortions of logic when asked whether we should rebuild as was, or design something contemporary instead, as the original architects had done in their time. Griffiths's ideas in such cases are simply liberating: 'What is the essence of a building? Is it in its substance and physical fabric, or in its design and form? ... Both the substance and the essence of a building is in its design, in its construction, and in its age, ... Morality has no bearing.'[9] In a comment piece for the *Architects' Journal* in 2018, he advocated the complete rebuilding of the Mackintosh Building exactly as it was before: 'Mackintosh's masterpiece is one of the great buildings of this country and must be rebuilt. Warsaw, Berlin, Dresden, St Petersburg demonstrate what can be done to rebuild great architecture catastrophically destroyed. The same can, and must, be done at the Mac.'[10]

The longevity and amazing diversity of work that Richard Griffiths Architects have produced, and the aged buildings they have rejuvenated, are testament to the respect in which they are held. Their deep knowledge of architectural history made them the ideal consultant to compile the Historic Impact Assessment for AHMM on the Tower Hamlets Civic Centre. Ⅎ

Notes
1. Richard Griffiths, *Old Buildings New Architecture*, Richard Griffiths Architects (London), 2019, p 105.
2. *Ibid*, p 9.
3. *Ibid*, p 11.
4. *Ibid*.
5. *Ibid*, p 13.
6. *Ibid*, p 87.
7. *Ibid*.
8. *Ibid*, p 167.
9. Richard White, 'Mac May Have to Be Pulled Down, Warn Experts', *Architects' Journal*, 18 June 2018: www.architectsjournal.co.uk/news/mac-may-have-to-be-pulled-down-warn-experts.
10. Ibid.

CONTRIBUTORS

Isabel Allen is Editorial Director of BEAM (Built Environment Architecture and Media). Her past roles include Editor of *The Architects' Journal*, co-founder and Design Director of HAB Housing, Communications Director for Design for London, and co-founder and Editor-in-Chief of *Citizen* magazine. She has curated and co-curated international exhibitions including the London pavilion at the Shanghai Expo in 2010 and the London exhibition for the 2019 Seoul Biennale. She is a member of the National Panel of the Civic Trust Awards, a Fellow of the Royal Society of Arts and an Honorary Fellow of the Royal Institute of British Architects (RIBA).

Frances Anderton is a writer, director and broadcaster. Previously she covered design and architecture for National Public Radio station KCRW in Los Angeles. She writes about West Coast design for many media outlets. Her publications include *Grand Illusion: A Story of Ambition, and its Limits, on LA's Bunker Hill* (2011), based on a studio she taught with Frank Gehry at the University of Southern California (USC) School of Architecture. She also produces podcasts and curates events and exhibitions; these have included 'Sink Or Swim: Designing for a Sea Change' (2014–15) about resilient architecture. Honours include the USC Architectural Guild's Esther McCoy Award for educating the public about architecture and urbanism.

Patrick Bellew is the founding director of Atelier Ten. He is a chartered building services engineer with nearly 40 years' experience of designing world-class environmental buildings. He is committed to the design of high-performance buildings and has written, lectured and talked extensively and globally on the subject. He has been a visiting lecturer and professor at the Yale University School of Architecture in New Haven, Connecticut, since 2000, and was a founding trustee of the UK Green Building Council from 2010 to 2017. A fellow of the UK's Royal Academy of Engineering, he was named a Royal Designer for Industry in 2010 by the Royal Society of Arts.

Peter Cook was a founder of Archigram in the late 1960s, taught at the Architectural Association in London from 1964 to 1990, and was a professor at the Städelschule, Frankfurt am Main, from 1984 to 2009. He was Professor and Chair of the Bartlett School of Architecture, University College London (UCL), from 1990 to 2006, and is a RIBA Royal Gold Medallist (with Archigram, 2007). He has authored nine books, and his drawings are in the collections of the Museum of Modern Art (MoMA) in New York, Deutsches Architekturmuseum (DAM) in Frankfurt, the Centre Pompidou and FRAC. His built works include the Kunsthaus Graz (2003) with Colin Fournier, and with his current practice, CRAB Studio, the Departments of Law and Central Administration at the University of Vienna (2013), Abedian School of Architecture at Bond University, Gold Coast, Australia (2014) and the Drawing Studio at the Arts University Bournemouth (2016). He was knighted in 2007 for services to architecture.

Martyn Evans spent 17 years with Cathedral Group, now U+I, including six years on the board before leaving to become the Development Director at the Dartington Hall Estate in Devon in 2016. He returned to U+I in 2019 as its Creative Director to deliver the strategy at the heart of its purpose-driven regeneration development portfolio. Martyn is also Deputy Chair of the London Festival of Architecture and founder of the Young Architects and Developers Alliance (YADA). He has been a jury member of the Architects' Journal Small Projects, the Architect of the Year, and New London Architecture (NLA) and Estates Gazette Awards, writes a regular column in *DBOnline* and contributes to the *Estates Gazette*.

Paul Finch is Programme Director of the World Architecture Festival (WAF) and Editorial Director of the *Architects' Journal* (*AJ*) and *Architectural Review* (*AR*). He previously edited *Building Design*, the *AJ* and *AR*, where he launched WAF in 2008. He was a founder commissioner at the Commission for Architecture & the Built Environment (CABE) in 1999, subsequently chairing its London Olympics design panel from 2005 to 2012. He became Chair in 2010, overseeing its merger with the Design Council in 2011, where he was Deputy Chair for three years. He holds an honorary doctorate from the University of Westminster and honorary fellowships from UCL and the RIBA. He is an honorary member of the British Council for Offices and the AA. He was awarded an OBE for services to architecture in 2002.

Hanif Kara is co-founder and Design Director of AKT II, a design-led structural and civil engineering firm based in London. He has gained international standing in the field of the built environment, through practice, pioneering research and education in interdisciplinary design. His work is widely published, and he is currently Professor in Practice of Architectural Technology at the Harvard University Graduate School of Design (GSD) in Cambridge, Massachusetts. His particular design-led approach and interest in innovative form, pushing material uses, sustainable construction and complex analysis methods have allowed him to work on numerous pioneering projects at the forefront of many challenges facing the built environment. His practice has won over 350 design awards over the last two decades, including the Stirling Prize on three occasions.

Jay Merrick was for several years the architecture critic for the *Independent* newspaper in London, and now writes on architecture and design for international publications including the *Architectural Review*, *Icon* and *Architects' Journal*. In his capacity as a consultant, he has written central texts for leading British and international architectural practices such as Grimshaw, Schmidt Hammer Lassen and Wilkinson Eyre. The subjects of his most recent monographs have been the Msheireb Museums in Doha, Eric Parry Architects, and the leading Mexican interior designer Gloria Cortina.

Joe Morris is the founding director of Morris+Company, an award-winning practice of architects, listeners, makers, curators, narrators, experimenters and innovators. As practice lead, he is an advocate for fair and transparent practice, and champions inclusivity and equality. He believes in open dialogue and critical debate, encouraging the broader company to take ownership of projects and develop their own careers and interests. He also believes in the potential for a more compassionate, sustainable global economy and seeks to raise awareness of these issues. He follows a strict vegan diet and advocates for others to do the same.

Morag Myerscough is an artist and designer who creates installations and immersive spatial artworks that transform places and champion community and public interaction. Her work is firmly rooted in a very personal experience of belonging, and never fails to charm, entice and encourage people to feel differently about their experience of where they are. Every artwork generates a very specific local response, which she uses to create community and build identity within a place. She is an Honorary Fellow of the RIBA and a Royal Designer for Industry.

Ellis Woodman is an architecture critic and curator, and the Director of the Architecture Foundation. He was formerly Editor of *Building Design*, and has written extensively for the *Daily Telegraph* as well as for a wide range of international periodicals. He has contributed texts to monographs on the work of architects including Peter Märkli, James Gowan, Craig Hamilton, Robbrecht en Daem, Biq, OFFICE Kersten Geers David Van Severen, Stephen Taylor, Carmody Groarke, Demetri Porphyrios and Sergison Bates.

Roger Zogolovitch is an architect and developer. He is the creative director of Solidspace, exploring new typologies of housing. Completion of the projects at 100 Union Street and 81–87 Weston Street, London, in collaboration with Simon Allford of AHMM, won the RIBA National award. He was chair of the client committee working on the masterplan for the regeneration of Burlington House that marked the 250th Anniversary of the Royal Academy of Arts. He is the author of *Shouldn't We All Be Developers?* (Artifice, 2015).

AHMM

Simon Allford studied architecture at the University of Sheffield and at the Bartlett School of Architecture, UCL, where he met his fellow founding partners of Allford Hall Monaghan Morris (AHMM). His work has won national and international awards for design and technological innovation, and has been widely published. Having recently stepped down from his longstanding role as Chair of the Architecture Foundation, he is now a trustee of the London School of Architecture (LSA), and has previously served as Honorary Treasurer and Secretary of the AA, as a trustee of the AA Foundation, and as Vice-President of the RIBA Education Committee. He has also been a visiting professor at the Bartlett and at Harvard GSD. He is president-elect of the RIBA and will be President from 2021 to 2023.

Jonathan Hall studied at Bristol University and the Bartlett, and holds Master's degrees in the History of Modern Architecture and Construction Law. His primary responsibility is the management of risk within the practice, and this includes leading both the technical and legal teams. This work is focused on directing and supporting the detailed management of projects and more generally on developing support systems that allow architects to focus effectively on the design and delivery of their projects. He co-chairs peer reviews of projects at key work stages, a role which underlines AHMM's belief in the interdependence of architectural excellence and prudent, professional management. He has been a professional examiner at a number of universities, and is currently the Part 3 External Examiner at the Bartlett for the 2020–24 period.

Paul Monaghan studied architecture at the University of Sheffield (from which he was awarded an honorary doctorate in 2018) and at the Bartlett. He led AHMM's work on the RIBA Stirling Prize-winning Burntwood School, as well as two other Stirling-shortlisted buildings: Westminster Academy and the Kentish Town Health Centre. In addition to his project work, he is a visiting professor at the Bartlett and Sheffield schools of architecture; he has also been Vice-Chair of the CABE Schools Design Review Panel, and was on the CABE National Design Review Panel. More recently he has been an adviser to the UK government's Building Better, Building Beautiful Commission. He chaired the RIBA awards panel until 2010, and was a judge for the Stirling Prize in 2016. He was appointed as the Liverpool City Region's first Design Champion in 2018.

Peter Morris studied architecture at the University of Bristol and at the Bartlett. As AHMM's Managing Director, his main focus is on the design and management of the practice itself, while as an architect he maintains a close working relationship with its work through critical review of all projects. This dual role acknowledges AHMM's belief in the interdependence of professional excellence and good business practice. He has also been responsible for the direction of various projects from inception through to completion, including several interventions at the Barbican Centre in London. His commitments outside the practice include acting as a member of the Royal Borough of Kensington and Chelsea's Architecture Appraisal Panel, and he is the Chair of the Old Street District voluntary business-led partnership.

What is *Architectural Design*?

Founded in 1930, *Architectural Design* (Δ) is an influential and prestigious publication. It combines the currency and topicality of a newsstand journal with the rigour and production qualities of a book. With an almost unrivalled reputation worldwide, it is consistently at the forefront of cultural thought and design.

Issues of Δ are edited either by the journal Editor, Neil Spiller, or by an invited Guest-Editor. Renowned for being at the leading edge of design and new technologies, Δ also covers themes as diverse as architectural history, the environment, interior design, landscape architecture and urban design.

Provocative and pioneering, Δ inspires theoretical, creative and technological advances. It questions the outcome of technical innovations as well as the far-reaching social, cultural and environmental challenges that present themselves today.

For further information on Δ, subscriptions and purchasing single issues see:

https://onlinelibrary.wiley.com/journal/15542769

Volume 90 No 2
ISBN 978 1119 555094

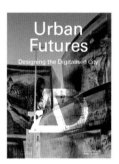

Volume 90 No 3
ISBN 978 1119 617563

Volume 90 No 4
ISBN 978 1119 576440

Volume 90 No 5
ISBN 978 1119 651581

Volume 90 No 6
ISBN 978 1119 685371

Volume 91 No 1
ISBN 978 1119 717669

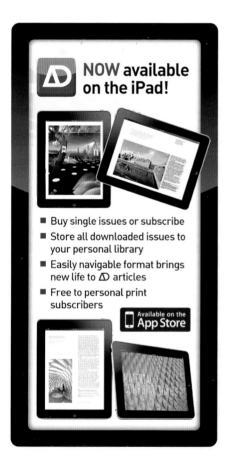